Champagne
COCKTAILS

Champagne COCKTAILS

ANISTATIA MILLER, JARED BROWN, & DON GATTERDAM

ReganBooks

An Imprint of HarperCollins*Publishers*

This book is gratefully dedicated to the first hopeless romantic who ever slipped a raspberry into a glass of Champagne

first edition

Designed by P.R. Brown @ Bau-Da Design Lab

0-06-039292-4

99 00 01 02 03 ❖/RRD 10 9 8 7 6 5 4 3 2 1

the Cocktail Menu

PREFACE

After completing *Shaken Not Stirred®: A Celebration of the Martini* (HarperPerennial, 1997), we dove back into our personal collection of antique bartending guides, history books, and volumes of trivia, looking for the origins of other classic cocktails. We furthered our investigations by contacting top barmen in New York, London, Seattle, Las Vegas, San Francisco, and Chicago. We tested the resulting recipes along with two dozen very brave volunteers.

Our never-ending search for the perfect cocktail has been a bit like a quest for the Grail: It's been a long, arduous search for a divine cup. Only ours might come on the rocks with a twist. The journey has taken us down some strange roads, past shooters, coolers, jelly shots, and a few too many umbrella drinks. Luckily, the road has also scaled some lofty pinnacles with names like Martini, Manhattan, classic Daiquiri, Mojito, and Sazerac, to name

○

I make wine for myself.
What I can't drink, I sell!

—Victor Lanson,
Lanson Champagne

just a few. But throughout it all, one cocktail has always towered far above the rest: the Champagne cocktail. It's the beverage of choice for the most important occasions, the most intimate moments, and the most celebratory toasts.

Other ingredients come alive in the presence of sparkling wine. Its effervescence and light, fresh flavors release the subtleties found in cognac, port, vodka, and even stout, without losing its own vaunted complexities. It easily creates "third" flavors: those much sought-after tastes in the best cocktails where the whole becomes greater than the sum of its elixirs.

Although we use the term "Champagne" throughout this book, we'll be the first to admit that in testing these recipes we used a wide variety of sparkling wines from around the world. These include spumantes and proseccos from Italy, cavas from Spain, German sekts (hey, get your mind out of the gutter!), and outstanding domestic sparkling wines from California and Washington.

INTRODUCTION

It's undeniable: There is no sexier drink than a Champagne cocktail. Refreshingly citrus drinks like Mimosas and Poinsettias turn brunch into an affair. A Moulin Rouge or a Kir Royale can help prolong lunch for hour after pleasant hour. No black-tie reception would be complete without silver trays bearing flights of crystal-clear Champagne cocktails. Before dinner, appetite-stimulating concoctions such as the Du Monde enliven rather than anesthetize the palate. And later in the evening, the rich tastes of port and Champagne combined in a Nelson's Blood make the perfect nightcap.

"But," you ask, "Isn't it sacrilege to use good sparkling wine in a cocktail?" Is it a sin to drive a Ferrari on the street? Ferraris, after all, are built for racing. No. It's not a sin. In fact, it's the ultimate luxury.

Would it offend the Champagne vintners? Roughly one out of every five bottles of Champagne consumed in France is poured into a cocktail. There

○
He who never takes risks, never gets to drink Champagne.

—Russian proverb

The pail is brought,
the ice is clinking
Round old Moët or
Veuve Clicquot.
This is what poets
should be drinking
And they delight
to see it flow.

—Alexander Pushkin
Eugene Onegin (1847)

CASSANDRA:

I believe I've never had
French Champagne before.

BENJAMIN:

Well, actually all
Champagne is French;
named after the region.
Otherwise, it's sparkling
white wine. Americans
don't recognize the con-
vention, so it becomes that
thing of calling all of their
sparkling white wines
Champagne even though by
definition they're not.

WAYNE:

Ah, yes. It's alot like Star
Trek: The Next Generation.
In many ways it's superior,
but will never be as
recognized as the original.

—*Wayne's World* (1992)

have been Champagne cocktails nearly as long as cocktails of any kind have been around. According to various sources, they were popular long before the Martini, the Manhattan, the Old Fashioned, or even the Julep were invented during the mid-1800s.

But it shouldn't be too surprising because Champagne, unlike other wines, has almost never been the unadulterated fruit of the grape. Early in its history, sugar and brandy were added during the manufacturing process to bring this effervescent libation to life. (Appropriately, the traditional Champagne Cocktail uses those exact same ingredients along with a dash of bitters and a lemon twist. Thus, the extra elements release the flavors which first made Champagne so wildly popular.) Nearly all sparkling wines produced these days (even the driest ones) are sweetened by varying degrees with additional sugar before they are bottled.

While sparkling wines are wonderful, sparkling-wine cocktails are far more personal. The wine itself celebrates the vintners' art, but the addition of flavor-enhancing ingredients allows us to participate in the creation of a broad collection of truly elegant drinks. Each glass becomes unique, contributing new subtleties to Champagne's complexities and tailoring each experience perfectly to fit any special moment.

This wine where foaming bubbles dance,
reflects the brilliant soul of France.

—Voltaire

The cuverie at Mumm's is where juices
are stored during the first stage of
fermentation.

Let's set the record

straight—Champagne is only made in France. Everything else is sparkling wine (which, by the way, can be truly excellent). So what made France's Champagne region the Champagne hot spot? Chalk. That's right. The stubs teachers use to write on black slate. The stark-white rock that greets you from England's southeastern shores when you cross the English Channel. It paved the roads that led to and from Rome, and those Roman highways and byways stretched out to remote places like Gaul (now Belgium, France, Germany, and part of northern Italy).

A Funny Thing Happened on the Way to Gaul

Emperor Julius Caesar began the memoirs of his Gallic conquest with a simple sentence that every Latin student learns in the first week of class: "Gaul as a whole consists of three separate parts: one is inhabited by the Belgae, another by the Aquitani, and the third by the people we call Gauls." Today, northeastern Aquitani is further divided into four departments, including Ardennes, Aube, Marne, and Haute-Marne. They are also known by a more familiar regional name: Champagne. Situated about 90 miles northeast of Paris, the Champagne-Ardennes district covers about 9,886 square miles, a little over twice the size of the state of Connecticut.

When the Romans first settled in Gaul circa 50 AD, they planted most of their prized vines in places like Bordeaux, Burgundy, and Loire, not on the dry chalk hillsides around the Plaine de Champagne. The district's chilly climate and thin, barren soil were considered better suited to corn. Not until around 276 AD did Roman Emperor Marcus Aurelius Probus grant the people of Champagne the right to plant grapevines once again.

Champagne's vineyards flourished after that. Wines made at the local Abbey de Saint Basles (which were made with grapes from the bishop of Reims' own vineyards) were said to tame even barbarians like Clovis, the Merovingian ruler of the Franks (who later converted

Bottles of Champagne stored in underground cellars at Louis Roederer.

to Christianity, though whether he did so to get more of the monks' wine is unknown).

Other monasteries popped up in the region during the seventh century, including Abbey d'Épernay, Abbey d'Hautvillers, and Abbey d'Avenay, so the number of local vineyards grew. Word about Champenois monasteries' libations spread, which kept the local wine makers busy harvesting, stomping, and fermenting.

The Holy Roman Emperor, good King Wenceslas—of Christmas carol fame—journeyed from his home in Bohemia to Reims in 1397. He had two goals: The first was to taste the region's wines, and the second was to sign peace agreements with King Charles VI. According to legend, once he reached Reims he was willing to sign almost anything as long as it didn't interrupt his drinking.

Adding a Sparkle to the Day

In 1668, a young, blind Benedictine monk named Dom Pierre Pérignon became the cellar master (and chief accountant) at the Abbey d'Hautvillers. The Champenois abbeys had already earned a reputation for producing not only the best rosés, honey-colored wines, and whites, but also a dubious local specialty: *vin blanc mousseux* (sparkling white wine) which was produced in one of two ways. The first method was a process called *méthode champenoise* (as documented by a British chemist named Christopher Merret in 1662). The second was a simpler procedure called *méthode ancestrale*, which simply entailed bottling the wine while it still contained yeast and sugar. However, both were considered to be somewhat foolish winemaking practices because sparkling wines tended to explode in the cellars. In fact, most people referred to these early sparkling wines as *vins diables* (devil wines) or *saute bouchons* (cork poppers).

It's been said that Champagne basically invented itself, and in many ways that statement is true. Champagne's short growing seasons, cold temperatures, and late harvests combined to start *vin blanc mousseux* bubbling. Bottled in the late fall after cold temperatures halted the fermentation (so that the fermentation did not finish before bottling), the wine would begin to ferment again in the spring inside the bottle. The pressure and bubbles are produced because yeasts— little microorganisms—eat sugar, and in turn produce alcohol and carbon dioxide. If they do this in a sealed bottle, the carbon dioxide can't escape, which creates natural carbonation.

Dom Pérignon didn't invent Champagne, but he did make Champagne better. When he gave up trying to rid the wine of bubbles, Pérignon learned that he could capture the effervescence (prevent it from exploding or escaping) by using strong British-made glass bottles that employed an iron-and-magnesium formula. The diligent Pérignon also reintroduced the ancient art of sealing the bottles with Spanish cork plugs instead of the standard oil-soaked hemp and wood bottle stoppers used by local *vin blanc mousseux* producers of the time. (According to one legend, he was inspired by the cork stoppers used in the water bottles of visiting Spanish monks.) He then took on the task of improving the local wines by creating a *cuvée* (blend) of black grapes gathered from a selection of Champenois vineyards.

Seeing Stars

Around 1813, Madame Barbe-Nicole Clicquot developed an important process in the making of Champagne—*remuage* (riddling). And she did it right in her dining room. Widowed at age twenty-seven, this young woman took over the business her late husband François had founded: a *maison de Champagne*. Better known in town as the Veuve Clicquot (the Widow Clicquot), she

worked closely with her cellar master Antoine Müller to refine these processes. In 1818, they shared their secrets on how to clear the cloudy sediments from Champagne. Madame Clicquot and Müller created the first *pupître* (riddling rack), by cutting holes into her dining table. She inserted the Champagne bottles at an angle, rotating them a quarter turn each day for two months—a process called *remuage*, or the "bottle dance." Then she opened each bottle upside down. By the time she could stop the flow with her thumb, the sediment had washed out. This method was a crude predecessor to *dégorgement*, freezing the neck and letting the pressure push the frozen sediment out, which wasn't invented until 1884, by another Frenchman, Armand Walfart (pronounced "val-far"). A mixture of wine, sugar, and sometimes brandy, called *liqueur d'expedition*, was then added to the bottle to increase the strength and sweetness of the flavor—a process which wine masters call *dosage*. Finally, the wine was recorked. This system helped the wine retain most of its bubbly carbon dioxide through the elimination of the decanting process used by most vintners.

O

In 1908, the first law was passed in France restricting the use of the name "Champagne" to sparkling wines that were grown and produced in the Vallée de la Marne and Aisne departments of the region. It took another nineteen years for wines produced in the Aube to be given the same Champagne a.o.c. (*appellation d'origine côntrolée*, or controlled origin of label).

During the early 1930s, an international agreement was signed by most of the world's sparkling wine producers, officially recognizing the name "Champagne" as referring to the French region that bears its name. (Deep in the throws of Prohibition, the United States was the only producer-nation that did not send delegates to this critical meeting.)

As David Niven poured himself a glass of Champagne, a fellow actor said, "I thought you had given up drinking." Niven replied, "But Champagne is not drinking."

How It's Made Today

Cheap sparkling wines can be produced in just a few months. However, better sparkling wines, like those made according to the *méthode champenoise* process, require at least eighteen months of meticulous processing and aging in the bottle to create their unique flavors and textures. Vintage Champagnes and sparkling wines take nearly four years to attain their vaunted status.

The process begins with the selection of the grapes. Since Dom Pérignon and his fellow monks developed the *cuvée* (blend), most Champagnes and sparkling wines combine juice from two varieties of black grapes (Pinot Noir and Pinot Meunier—a cousin of Noir which was discovered during the sixteenth century) and one variety of white grape (Chardonnay).

At harvest time, the grapes are picked by hand so that all of the malformed, rotten, bruised, or split fruit can be discarded. The grapes are pressed gently in huge wooden presses to avoid crushing the skins, which would impart red color into the delicate, pale juice. Then, it's time to make wine.

Assemblage: Each type of juice is fermented naturally in separate vats until early spring, when each has turned to dry wine. The various wines are then blended into a *cuvée*. (A 65 percent black grape

It's been estimated that two billion bottles of sparkling wine are consumed each year, and 12 to 15 percent of that comes from Champagne.

Madame Lily Bollinger—one of Champagne's most famous widows—toured her vineyards by bicycle almost daily, well beyond her eightieth birthday. In 1961, she was asked by a newspaper reporter when she personally drank Champagne. She replied: "I drink it when I'm happy and when I'm sad. Sometimes I drink it when I'm alone. When I have company I consider it obligatory. I trifle with it if I'm not hungry and drink it when I am. Otherwise I never touch it—unless I'm thirsty."

Dom Pérignon called out to his assistants the first time he tasted the fruits of his labors: "Come quickly, I'm drinking stars."

to 35 percent white grape ratio is common, but various producers have closely guarded secret proportions.)

Tirage: Sugar and yeast are added when the *cuvée* is bottled. This initiates a second fermentation called the *prise de mousse* (creation of the effervescence). This increases the alcohol content by one degree and adds enough carbon dioxide to establish six atmospheres of pressure.

The second fermentation is over within a month. However, French law dictates that even non-vintage bottles must be stored in a cellar for one to three years, allowing the wines to mature and mellow. During this time, the wine is said to "rest on its lees" (the sediment left from the fermentation). Many flavor characteristics and complexities are attributed to the lees.

Remuage and Dégorgement: After a nice long rest, the Champagne is rotated to move the sediment to the neck where it's frozen and removed. The bottle is then recorked and the process is complete.

All that time and effort ends in a pop of the cork. But the pop is also a beginning, because there are thousands of ways to enjoy sparkling wines, and hundreds of cocktails to be made.

This is the land that produces the drink that lubricates the world's celebrations. It even boasts villages with accidentally appropriate names like Dizy and Bouzy.
—**Kevin Connolly, BBC correspondent**

CHAPTER 2

fizz ed

MIXOLOGY FUNDAMENTALS

One Champagne expert remarked to us, "Why do people insist on making cocktails with Champagne? You don't hear about cocktails made with Bordeaux or other fine wines!" (Actually, there are many wonderful wine-based cocktails. Cold Duck (*see page 68*), before it became associated with plastic corks and leopard-print interiors, was a fine cocktail combining equal parts Champagne and red Bordeaux.) However, this same expert readily acknowledged that the French consume as much as 20 percent of their own Champagne in cocktails.

Why do people make Champagne cocktails? It's simple: The cocktail itself is the apex of the mixologist's craft, while Champagne is the pinnacle of the winemaker's art. These are the best—there are no finer cocktails on earth. There is no beverage more decadent, more pleasurable, or more inspiring than a perfectly prepared Champagne cocktail.

The Basics

Champagne cocktails require only a few essential implements. You'll need an ice bucket, a clean bar towel, a calibrated shot glass, a bar spoon, Champagne flutes, ice, a paring knife, and a cutting board. These particular cocktails are rarely shaken—or stirred for that matter. The bubbles do a surprisingly good job of mixing the cocktail without assistance. Besides, undue agitation causes Champagne to quickly lose its sparkle. However, a shaker or mixing glass and a strainer are still handy tools for combining and chilling other cocktail ingredients before the Champagne is added.

Liqueurs and other ingredients should be chilled in the refrigerator for at least twenty minutes before use. Hard spirits such as vodka or gin can be stored in the freezer. The reason is simple. When you add cold liquor to a Champagne cocktail, it stays chilled longer. (Champagne is considered to be at its best around 44°F. A Champagne cocktail containing thoroughly chilled liqueurs and spirits seems to rise from about 40°F to 48°F if consumed at a normal pace, according to our measurements.)

As the average Champagne cocktail requires 4 oz. of Champagne, and a 750 ml. bottle holds 33.8 oz., each bottle makes roughly eight cocktails. At three drinks per person for a cocktail party (or more, depending on your guests), it would take two bottles for every five people.

Throughout this book, we'll refer to measurements by their popular names. A conversion chart to ounces and metric units follows:

POPULAR NAME	OUNCES	METRIC
1 dash	0.021 oz.	0.833 ml.
1 teaspoon (tsp.)	0.125 oz.	4.92 ml.
1 splash	0.25 oz.	7.5 ml.
1 tablespoon (tbs.)	0.50 oz.	14.786 ml.
1 pony	1 oz.	29.573 ml.
1 jigger	1.5 oz.	44.36 ml.
1 wineglass	4 oz.	118.292 ml.
1 flute	6 oz.	177.438 ml.
1 coupe	6 oz.	177.438 ml.
1 split (qtr. bottle)	6.3 oz.	187 ml.
1 cup	8 oz.	236.584 ml.
1 half bottle	12.7 oz.	375 ml.
1 pint	16 oz.	473.2 ml.
1 bottle	25.3 oz.	750 ml.
1 quart	32 oz.	946.4 ml.
1 magnum (2 bottles)	50.8 oz.	1.5 litres
1 jeroboam (4 bottles)	101.6 oz.	3 litres
1 rehoboam (6 bottles)	147 oz.	4.5 litres
1 methuselah (8 bottles)	196 oz.	6 litres
1 salmanazar (12 bottles)	304.8 oz.	9 litres
1 balthazar (16 bottles)	406.4 oz.	12 litres
1 nebuchadnezzar (20 bottles)	508 oz.	15 litres

RICK (to Ilse):

Henri wants us to finish this bottle, and then three more. He says he'll water his garden with Champagne before he'd let the Germans drink it.

—*Casablanca* (1942)

Why have a Champagne cocktail before dinner, instead of a Martini, Manhattan, or other high-proof cocktail? Champagne cocktails contain less alcohol. They don't anesthetize the taste buds, allowing diners to taste and enjoy their dinner to the fullest. Stronger aperitifs should be reserved as overtures to airplane and hospital food, or they should be consumed long before dinner. That's why happy hour's at five and dinner's at eight. It gives your taste buds a chance to sober up.

The large bottles were named by the wine bottlers themselves, after Babylonian kings like Balthazar who made a great feast and "drank wine before the thousands [of guests]" and Biblical characters such as Methuselah, who was known for his longevity. (This is appropriate, as larger bottles take longer to age; thus they have greater longevity.)

Whatever Pops Your Cork

Everyone's seen at least one Champagne shower: the victorious team at an Indy 500 race spraying each other with magnums of bubbly, or the winning team at the World Series showering the locker room. This is how *not* to open a bottle of Champagne. There's an old saying about opening Champagne: "The ear's loss is the palate's gain." To put it less poetically, Champagne has a limited amount of sparkle. If more goes into making a bang, then less goes into the glass.

An ancient *sommelier* (waiter in charge of wine) once explained that Champagne is opened in sixes. Once the foil is removed, it takes six half-twists to remove the wire. (Some of the most respected writers on wine have called the wire which secures the cork: the "cage,"

Nearly every Champagne bottle has a punt—that odd divot in the bottom of the bottle. It's considered proper etiquette to pour Champagne by placing your thumb in the punt and fanning your fingers along the lower part of the bottle. However, the punt's true functional origins are shrouded in mystery.

Was it designed to make bottles appear larger to consumers? No, the difference in bottle sizes with or without a punt is imperceptible. When bottles were hand-blown, a narrow iron rod was affixed to the bottom of the bottle after it was blown, allowing the glassblower to finish the neck. This rod was called a *pontil* or punt.

The most plausible theory is that the punt makes the bottle more sturdy. Before punts were added, riddling was about as risky as tap dancing in a minefield. The people who turned the bottles wore fencing masks and chest protectors. The punt redirects the pressure away from the bottom. If a bottle explodes while being riddled, the sides give way instead of the bottom.

There we were on New Year's Eve, standing in a batting cage with a basket full of chilled Champagne bottles and a radar gun. It was time to find out just how fast a popped cork travels. It didn't take long to discover that no matter how close or how fast the cork passed by the radar gun, it was completely undetectable. Now if only we could find a cork-bodied Porsche.

Car tire = 28-36 psi (pounds per sq. inch) Mountain bike tire = 45-60 psi Champagne= 95 psi

How much gas is there in a bottle of Champagne? Set a full bottle on the counter, then set five or six empty bottles next to it. The volume of those extra bottles is about equal to the amount of gas in the full bottle.

There is a wide range of great sparkling wines made in places outside of France's Champagne region, such as Italy (spumante and prosecco), Germany (sekt), and North America (sparkling wine).

Expensive glasses are actually better for serving sparkling wine. Aside from crystal's superlative look and feel, it also has a slightly rougher surface, allowing bubbles to gain more minute footholds. This provides the wine with the classic look of many fine streams of tiny bubbles.

A cork is a wonderful memento for any special occasion. It's surprisingly easy to write on them, and inscribing the date and a message turns a cork into a keepsake.

the "bale," the "basket," the "wire," the "wire hood," the "wire straps," the "wire muzzle," and "that wire thing." Its French name is *muselet,* pronounced "mew-suh-lay".) Then, make six gentle twists of the bottle while holding the cork firmly to bring up the cork without a pop, just a hiss. But let's face it, without some pop what's the fun? A slight pop with just a wisp of vapor—rather than a fountain all over the living room—doesn't seem to harm the wine.

One word of caution: Never use a corkscrew to open any bottle of sparkling wine. The corkscrew and cork will likely come out of the bottle like a deadly projectile from a Bruce Lee movie. And another word of caution: Beware of the cork. Its muzzle velocity has been estimated at upwards of sixty miles per hour. Plus, the record distance for a popped cork is roughly one hundred feet. So watch where you're aiming that little plug. Don't point it at your head, your guests (even ones you don't like), your pets, or your cherished collection of Champagne flutes.

A budding young inventor named James Sweed recently developed a safety device intended for opening Champagne bottles which won him a finalist's spot in a Hammacher Schlemmer inventors competition. A latex affair that vaguely resembles a mini-condom, the invention fits over the top of the bottle so the force of the cork is dissipated in a protective housing. But isn't the risk part of the thrill? Isn't safe sex enough? Do we have to have safe romance, too?

One more word of caution: Never stick a bottle of Champagne in the freezer to chill. In rampant defiance of everything you learned (or slept through) in high-school chemistry, water and wine expand rapidly when they go from liquid to solid. Champagne is already under a lot of pressure, so the results can be atomic. If your date is arriving in ten minutes, set the bottle in an ice bucket surrounded by a mix of ice, cold water, and a little salt. Give it a gentle spin every few minutes and it'll be perfectly chilled and ready to open by the time you've hung up his/her coat and introduced him/her to your pet goldfish.

My Cup Runneth Over

Long before the birth of the coupe (which, legend has it, was modeled after Marie Antoinette's breasts, at her request, *see page 54*), Champagne was served in taller, more slender glasses, much like the Champagne flutes and tulips that are popular today. Flutes and tulips highlight the bubbles, concentrating them in the center and giving them

There comes a time in every woman's life when the only thing that helps is a glass of Champagne.
—Bette Davis,
Old Acquaintance (1943)

I like my woman warm and my Champagne cold.
—Groucho Marx

the longest possible distance to travel through the wine. They also reduce the exposed surface area, so that the wine keeps its fizz longer. The Riedel company—producer of some of the best-designed crystal glasses available—recommends serving four to five ounces of brut Champagne in eleven-ounce flutes, allowing the aromas of the wine to rise to your nose. Some of the best flutes have a small dot called a "fizz mark" etched into the bottom of the bowl, providing a rough surface that generates a continuous focused stream of bubbles. With glass etching tools available at many hardware stores, you could even make a small mark in the bottom of your own Champagne glasses. (Isn't that what Martha Stewart would do?)

Shake It Up

Of all the ingredients combined for most Champagne cocktails, the Champagne is added last, after everything but the garnish. This minimizes the time between pouring and serving. It's one of the rules of good barmanship: ingredients go into a drink via monetary value. In other words, ice or sugar goes in first, juices and liqueurs go in second, hard spirits are third, and Champagne goes in last.

To pour Champagne into a cocktail, first pour a small amount of Champagne into the flute. It will foam up and then settle. Once it calms down, the rest of the Champagne should go in easily without a lot of foam

(provided the flute is clean and the Champagne is well-chilled and poured gently). If excess foam still bubbles up, tilt the glass and pour down the edge. If you can't get the hang of it, practice. Even if no one's looking, you can't simply suck the foam off the top and stand there looking like a rabid chipmunk until the bubbles settle out of your cheeks.

To Twist or Not to Twist

Traditional Champagne cocktail recipes often call for an orange or lemon twist. But these little strips of peel give Champagne bubbles a lot of rough surface to hang onto, allowing them to escape more rapidly and flattening the drink. You can improve your cocktail's staying power by rubbing the rim of the glass with the twist, wringing it over the cocktail, and then discarding the twist, or balancing it on the rim. If you truly prefer to place the twist in the cocktail, then use a short piece that will have space to float to the top where it will do the least damage to your drink.

If you are garnishing with fresh berries, freeze them first. Obviously, this makes them colder, so that they don't warm your drink. But freezing also breaks down berries' cell walls, releasing the juice. They'll keep their shape and appearance if you put them in the drink while they're still frozen. As they thaw in the cocktail, their juices will come pouring out.

Frosting the Flute

With a little practice, it's quite easy to create a perfect sugar rim every time (of course, you might say that it's also quite easy—with a little practice—to float nine layers of liqueurs in a *pousse café*). But seriously, all it takes is two small dishes and

O

3 CHAPTER

i get a kick out of you

CLASSIC CHAMPAGNE COCKTAILS

In the May 13, 1806 issue of an American magazine called *The Balance*, the cocktail was described as: "a stimulating liquor, composed of spirits of any kind, sugar, water, and bitters—it is vulgarly called bittered sling, and is supposed to be an excellent electioneering potion." It didn't take long for sparkling wine to become a popular ingredient in this very American drink, creating the ultimate elixir—the Champagne cocktail.

In his novel *Innocents Abroad* (1869), Mark Twain wrote:

We ferreted out another French imposition—a frequent sign to this effect: "All manner of American drinks artistically prepared here."

We procured the services of a gentlemen experienced in the nomenclature of the American bar, and moved upon the works of one of those impostors. A bowing, aproned Frenchman skipped forward and said: "Que voulez les messieurs?"

I do not know what "Que voulez les messieurs?" means but such was his remark.

Our general said: "We will take a whiskey straight."

[A stare from the Frenchman.]

"Well, if you don't know what that is, give us a Champagne cock-tail."

Champagne Cocktail

As served at the Connaught Hotel, London, England

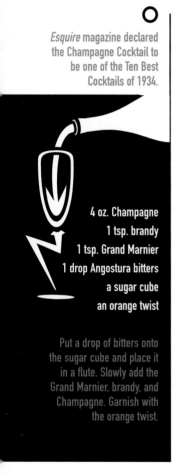

Esquire magazine declared the Champagne Cocktail to be one of the Ten Best Cocktails of 1934.

4 oz. Champagne
1 tsp. brandy
1 tsp. Grand Marnier
1 drop Angostura bitters
a sugar cube
an orange twist

Put a drop of bitters onto the sugar cube and place it in a flute. Slowly add the Grand Marnier, brandy, and Champagne. Garnish with the orange twist.

Author John F. Mariani postulates that "since the 1870s a mixture using Champagne or sparkling wine was called a 'Champagne cocktail.'" It's been served in London's fanciest hotels since the turn of the century. From the Connaught and the Ritz hotels to the Savoy, Champagne cocktails have become venerated traditions. The Savoy employed the great chef and father of French cuisine, Auguste Escoffier, who was instrumental in educating the posh British public to the joys of Champagne ever since his arrival in 1889. Escoffier featured a Champagne cocktail on his Champagne list, despite his abhorrence of consuming *les cocktails* before dinner. During the 1920s, the Savoy further advanced the Champagne cocktail when it commissioned the services of renowned mixologist Harry Craddock. This barman topped his classic bubbling cocktail with an ice cube, a lemon twist, and a large orange slice.

A number of unique variations were born across the pond from the Champagne cocktail's American home. Craddock developed the Alfonso during the 1920s, substituting Secrestat Bitters for Angostura bitters and Dubonnet for the

O

Lillet is an apéritif wine produced from a careful blend of fine Bordeaux wines, enhanced by liqueurs that are crafted from a variety of fruits, such as sweet and bitter oranges from Spain, Morocco, Haiti, and South America, as well as chinchona (a.k.a. quinine). A tree bark that was originally added to liqueurs and sweetened sparkling water to convince soldiers to take their malaria medication, quinine turned out to impart a wonderful flavor and is still the predominant flavor in tonic water. Originally called Kina Lillet, the name was shortened to Lillet to avoid imitation. (In French, quinine is abbreviated "kina.")

Lillet Blond (or Blanc) has subtle flavors of honey, orange, lime, and mint. Lillet Rouge is spicier, laced with essences of vanilla and berries. Blond replaces vermouth in the Vesper— James Bond's classic Martini—as described in Ian Fleming's novel *Casino Royale*. Although they're both delicious straight or in Champagne cocktails, we discovered that Lillet is a truly superlative replacement for vermouth anytime.

familiar brandy. Harry's Pick-Me-Up replaced the bitters-soaked sugar cube with grenadine syrup. Today, the Chemin de Fer in Eureka, California, switches the brandy with Lillet Blanc apéritif wine.

Even before the classic Champagne Cocktail, there was another form of Champagne libation that gained wide repute. Filled with anything from fruits and strong liqueurs to cucumber slices and fresh herbs, Champagne punches have been around almost as long as the wine itself. The Bombay Punch, for example, was a hit among British officers stationed in India during the "Great Mutiny" of the mid-1800s. Champagne Cups were a featured item in Mrs. Beeton's *Book of Household Management* (1861). During the Second World War, Champagne Cups and Champagne Apricot were hot topics in stateside establishments such as Trader Vic's famous, dimly-lit Polynesian palace located deep in the heart of Oakland, California. Known for creating memorable rum concoctions, Trader Vic himself once admitted that his favorite nightcap was Champagne: "preferably after I'm already in bed—to hell with that hot milk stuff!"

A rather drunk customer was downing cups of Champagne Punch and wishing everyone a happy New Year as he staggered around the bar. Finally, the bartender pulled him aside and told him it was the middle of March.

"What am I going to tell my wife?" the man replied. "I've never stayed out this late before!"

The Savoy's Champagne Cocktail was very similar. Put 1 drop Angostura bitters onto a sugar cube and place it in a flute with an ice cube. Slowly add 5 oz. Champagne. Garnish with both a lemon twist and an orange slice. It's also served this way at the Gerard Lounge in Vancouver. (An early American version—called a London Special—replaced the Angostura bitters with Peychaud bitters.)

The Bellagio Resort & Casino in Las Vegas serves a Champagne Celebration. Put 1 drop of Peychaud bitters onto a raw sugar cube and place it in a flute. Add 1 splash of each: brandy and Cointreau. Slowly fill the flute with 5 oz. Champagne. Garnish with an orange twist.

Chemin de Fer in Eureka, California serves a Champagne Cocktail with an edge. Put 1 drop of Angostura bitters onto a sugar cube and place it in a flute. Add 1 splash Lillet Blanc. Slowly fill the flute with 5 oz. Champagne. Garnish with a lemon peel and an orange slice.

The Alfonso served at London's Savoy Hotel is a sweeter variation. Put 2 drops Secrestat bitters onto a sugar cube and place it in a flute along with an ice cube and 1 oz. Dubonnet. Slowly add 4 oz. Champagne. Garnish with a lemon twist.

Harry's Pick-Me-Up served at the Savoy Hotel mixes 1 tsp. grenadine syrup with the juice from half a lemon and 1 oz. brandy in a shaker filled with ice. Strain into a flute. Slowly add 4 oz. Champagne. Garnish with a lemon twist.

Traditional party-sized Bombay Punch mixes 1 qt. brandy, 1 qt. sherry, 4 oz. maraschino liqueur, 4 oz. curaçao, 4 qts. Champagne, 2 qts. sparkling mineral water in a punch bowl. Stir gently, garnish with slices of seasonal fruits, and set the punch bowl on a bed of cracked ice.

The Champagne Punch created by the Savoy's Harry Craddock combines 8 oz. confectioners' sugar, 2 qts. Champagne, 1 qt. sparkling mineral water, 4 oz. brandy, 4 oz. maraschino liqueur, and 4 oz. curaçao in a punch bowl. Stir gently, decorate with slices of seasonal fruits, and set the punch bowl on a bed of cracked ice.

James Beard's Champagne Punch mixes 8 tbs. sugar, 4 oz. lemon juice, 16 oz. orange juice, 2 bottles cognac, 16 oz. Cointreau, 4 bottles Champagne, and the grated peel from 4 lemons in a punch bowl. Stir gently, garnish with cucumber slices, and set the punch bowl on a bed of cracked ice.

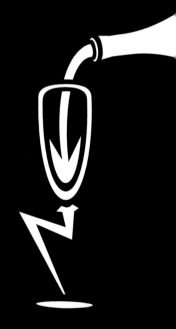

The Pink Champagne Cocktail served at the Hotel du Cap during the Cannes Film Festival (for $25 per flute) combines 1 tsp. brandy, 1 tsp. Grand Marnier, and 5 oz. rosé Champagne poured over a bitters-soaked sugar cube.

the Champagne Cup served at the original Trader Vic's is made in party-sized portions. Fill a large glass pitcher halfway with cracked ice. Cut 1 whole orange and half a lemon into thin slices. Add these to the pitcher along with 3 pineapple slices. Pour in 2 oz. brandy, 2 oz. maraschino liqueur, and 1 splash chartreuse. Chill for about two hours. Just before serving, slowly add 1 bottle Champagne. Serve in flutes decorated with pineapple, orange, and lemon slices.

Mrs. Beeton's Champagne Cup (circa 1861, England) combines 1 bottle Champagne, 2 bottles mineral water, 1 oz. curaçao or brandy, 2 tbs. confectioners' sugar, 1 lb. crushed ice, and 1 sprig fresh borage (a European herb). Serve in chilled silver cups garnished with sprigs of fresh borage.

The Savoy's Champagne Cup mixes 1 tbs. confectioners' sugar, 4 oz. brandy, 2 oz. curaçao, 1 oz. maraschino liqueur, 1 oz. Grand Marnier, and 1 qt. Champagne in a large pitcher. Garnish with 4 ice cubes, orange and pineapple slices, a very thin cucumber slice, and 4 sprigs fresh peppermint. Serve in flutes and garnish with orange twists.

An off-the-wall dessert cocktail called the Soyer-au-Champagne—also created by Craddock—combines 1 oz. vanilla ice cream, 2 dashes maraschino syrup, 2 dashes curaçao, and 2 dashes brandy in a flute. Stir well, slowly add 4 oz. Champagne and garnish with a fresh strawberry.

Craddock's Blue Train Special is another party-sized treat. Fill a shaker with cracked ice. Add 4 oz. brandy and 4 oz. pineapple juice. Shake and then add 12 oz. Champagne. Stir the contents very gently, then strain and pour into 6 flutes. Garnish with a pineapple slice in each glass.

The Champagne Apricot served at the original Trader Vic's in Oakland was an entertaining presentation. Put peeled apricots (fresh or canned and drained) into the freezer overnight. Place one frozen apricot into a coupe. Add 1 oz. Southern Comfort and 1 tsp. shaved ice, then slowly pour 4 oz. Champagne.

Lola's at Century House in Vancouver serves a Miss Scarlet which simply pairs 1 oz. Southern Comfort with 3 oz. Champagne in a flute.

Do I like Champagne? Ah, no, listen, that is a very personal question and one that I am not at liberty to answer... A less intimate question, yes. You should have asked me when I last made love, for example. You should have asked me when I last made love and enjoyed it.

—Henri Cartier-Bresson
(in response to a telephone survey)

Bellini

Created by Giuseppe Cipriani at Harry's Bar, Venice, Italy

Giuseppe Cipriani was a bartender at the Hotel Europa in Venice around 1929. One day, an American millionaire named Harry Pickering walked into the bar in a melancholic mood. He'd been sent on a voyage with his aunt to dry out, but word made it back to the states that he had been sipping his way through Cipriani's repertoire of dry Martinis and other inebriating delights. So the young man's pocket money had been cut off that morning.

Pickering asked the bartender if he would loan him the money to pay his hotel bill, his bar tab, and his ticket home—around 10,000 lire ($5,000). Cipriani had to discuss it with his wife. After all, he wasn't a rich man. But soon he obliged his good customer.

Not certain he would ever see his life savings again, Cipriani was relieved to see Harry stroll into the hotel bar again two years later. Pickering ordered a drink and handed the barman his 10,000 lire. "To show you my appreciation," the young man said, "here's 40,000 more, enough to open a bar. We'll call it Harry's Bar."

Open for business since May 13, 1931, Cipriani and Pickering's establish-

**1 oz. white peach purée
4 oz. Prosecco
(a dry Italian sparkling wine)**

Purée fresh peach slices in a blender or food processor (or buy a can of Kerr's Peach Nectar at the grocery store). Adjust the sweetness with a little sugar syrup, if desired. Refrigerate the purée until it's ice cold. Spoon the purée into a chilled shaker or mixing glass, then pour in the Prosecco. Stir gently and serve in a flute.

NURSE:

What do you want?

PATSY:

More Champagne, darling.

FLEUR:

Make mine a Buck's Fizz.

CATRIONA:

And some nibbles.

—"Hospital"
Absolutely Fabulous (1994)

Kilgore Trout once wrote a short story which was a dialogue between two pieces of yeast. They were discussing the possible purposes of life as they ate sugar and suffocated in their own excrement. Because of their limited intelligence, they never came close to guessing that they were making Champagne.

—Kurt Vonnegut,
Breakfast of Champions

ment has served the greats of the art and literary world including Noël Coward, Arturo Toscanini, Ernest Hemingway, and Humphrey Bogart. Harry's Bar has been frequented by the kings of Spain, Greece, and Yugoslavia. It was even pressed into service as a mess hall for German troops in 1943.

Shortly after Harry's Bar opened, Cipriani developed his signature drink. The Bellini was originally a summertime refresher, a 3-to-1 blend of icy-cold white peach purée shaken lightly with cold Prosecco (a dry Italian sparkling wine). This thirst-quenching combination was not officially christened until 1948. That's when it was named in honor of the early Renaissance artist Giovanni Bellini, whose work was the subject of a major exhibition displayed in Venice that same year.

So what did Harry's Bar do during the winter when white peaches were no longer in season? Well, customers did ask for Cipriani's other creations: the Montgomery (a 15-to-1 gin Martini), the Doge (a 2-to-1 gin Martini made with sweet Italian vermouth), and his version of the Cardinale (a blend of gin, Campari, and dry vermouth, which is not to be confused with a kir-style cocktail of the same name made with red burgundy wine and crème de cassis). But their favorite

Monzu in Manhattan serves a Bellinisimo which combines 2 oz. pear purée and 1 oz. raspberry liqueur in a flute. Gradually add 4 oz. Prosecco.

The Harry's Bar Mimosa combines 1 oz. fresh orange juice, 1 oz. tangerine juice, and 3 oz. Champagne, garnished with an orange wedge.

The Buck's Fizz served at the Savoy Hotel mixes 2 oz. fresh orange juice with 3 oz. Champagne, garnished with an orange wedge.

During the 1950s, Americans were sampling a Champagne Buck, which mixes 1 oz. dry gin, 1 splash cherry brandy, and 1 splash orange juice in a shaker filled with ice. Strain into a cocktail glass and slowly add 2 oz. Champagne.

According to the December 1997 issue of her magazine, Martha Stewart makes a Blood Orange Champagne Cocktail. It's a Mimosa that replaces the regular orange juice with this exotic fruit.

Lola's at the Century House makes The Copa which concocts 1 oz. fresh orange juice, 1 splash Cointreau, and 4 oz. Champagne.

The Tiziano served at Harry's Bar combines 1 oz. uva fragola grape juice (if this isn't available, you can use white grape juice) and 4 oz. Champagne.

The Rossini served at Harry's Bar mixes 1 oz. fresh strawberry purée with 4 oz. Prosecco in a flute.

The Playboy Club's Jo's Collins mixes 3 oz. Champagne, 1 oz. peach liqueur, 2 oz. fresh orange juice, and 1 splash 7-Up.

The Ritz Hotel in London serves the César Ritz (named after its founder), combining 1 splash of each: armagnac, peach liqueur, and grenadine with 4 oz. Champagne.

alternative was an orange creation that he called a Mimosa, a drink that was said to have been sipped in France before the 1920s. There are a number of interesting tales surrounding this popular twentieth-century brunch apéritif, a variation of which is called a Buck's Fizz in Great Britain.

Named after Buck's—a smart gentlemen's club situated on Clifford Street in London's pricey Mayfair district—the libation was introduced to club members during the 1920s. The club's founder was thirty-nine-year-old Captain Herbert John Buckmaster, who had divorced actress Gladys Cooper in 1921. Fond of hosting friends (many of them theater and film folk) and club members for rounds of golf, Buckmaster insisted on bringing his personal barman, Mr. McGarry, along to provide refreshments. During one of these sojourns, a member of the party asked McGarry to mix a peach-and-Champagne cocktail which he had tasted while on the continent (more than likely at Venice's Hotel Europa). Since there wasn't any fresh peach juice readily available, the mixologist made the drink with orange juice, Champagne, plus two additional ingredients which the current club secretary, Captain Peter Murison, says are only known by the establishment's barman and are kept secret from the outside world. However, we did discover a cocktail called a Champagne Buck in an early 1950s American cocktail guide that combines dry gin, cherry brandy, orange juice, and Champagne. Neverthless, the Buck's Fizz (minus its two secret ingredients) is served throughout the British Isles and is even available prebottled at any Marks & Spencer food shop. Despite its popularity in England, the Buck's Fizz seemed to remain a European secret for quite a while before it immigrated to America, where it became a Mimosa.

According to another account, the Mimosa was invented (or perhaps introduced to the States) by British film director Alfred Hitchcock at financier Louis Lourie's table in San Francisco's second oldest restaurant: Jack's. For fifty-two years, Louis had a daily reservation for ten, and the list of his guests reads like a who's who of celebrities and power-brokers. Sometime in the 1940s or 1950s, the rotund British director joined the fray. When the discussion turned to hangovers (which, apparently, a few attendees were suffering from), Champagne was added to Jack's fresh-squeezed orange juice as a palliative, and the resulting cocktail was dubbed the Mimosa.

Though he's better known for inventing pasteurization in 1867, Louis Pasteur became the first scientist to explain fermentation. Perhaps milk wasn't his favorite beverage after all.

Scientists at the University of West Ontario, Canada, discovered that the flavonoids in orange juice effectively inhibited the growth of cancer cells when combined with the antioxidant quercetin, which—though their study failed to mention it—is found in high doses in wine (including Champagne).

Legend has it that the "cocktail hour" (which eventually became happy hour) was born during Prohibition. Manhattan speakeasy owners had a deal with the local police: places like "21" wouldn't open their doors until 6 PM. But one establishment—Tony's at 42 East 53 St.—pushed these delicate boundaries, defying convention and openly serving pre-dinner cocktails between 4 PM and 6 PM.

Black Velvet

As served at The Savoy Hotel, London, England

6 oz. stout
6 oz. Champagne

Pour the stout into a chilled, tall 14 oz. glass. Then carefully add the Champagne.

Playwright and critic George Bernard Shaw once said: "Not everybody is strong enough to endure life without an anesthetic. Drink probably averts more gross crime than it causes." This Irishman who gained his fame in London also claimed to be a "beer teetotaler, not a Champagne teetotaler" because he didn't like beer. However, most of his fellow countrymen never took any oath of sobriety (or preference) because it meant denying themselves one of England's finest contributions to the world of drinking: a Black Velvet. The libation was said to be invented at Brooks's Club in London, in 1861, while the nation was grieving over the death of Prince Albert. The club steward decided that even the Champagne served should be in mourning, so he added Guinness stout to give it an appropriately sober hue.

An even balance of rich, frothy stout and light, fizzy Champagne—this is a happy marriage. Stout reveals Champagne's delicious, savory, biscuity tones, while it gains a wonderfully soft texture. The Black Velvet has also been deemed by some experts as one of the finest hangover cures ever invented. The barley-based B vitamins in the stout and natural carbonation from both liquids helps the body repair itself after a long night of merrymaking. (And the hair-of-the-dog does keep the pain away for a while.)

EDWARD CARSON:

Do you drink Champagne yourself?

OSCAR WILDE:

Yes; iced Champagne is a favorite drink of mine—strongly against my doctor's orders.

EDWARD CARSON:

Never mind your doctor's orders.

OSCAR WILDE:

I never do.

—Transcript of testimony given during Wilde's prosecution of the Marquess of Queensbury for criminal libel (April 4, 1895).

Leave it to the brew-crazy Brits to marry Champagne to their beloved stouts. The outcome is a creamy rich, savory cocktail which pairs well with (surprise, surprise) British cuisine: dishes like lamb and ale pie, prime rib, and Beef Wellington. Some great stouts to try include: Guinness (Ireland), Samuel Smith's Oatmeal Stout (UK), Murphy's (Ireland), and Boddington (UK).

SIR CHARLES LYTTON:

Have a glass of Champagne. Does wonders for extremists.... It's been known to launch some lasting friendships.

—*The Pink Panther* (1964)

STEFAN:

Now we can't be too serious this early in the morning—at least, not without a glass of Champagne. Won't take a minute. Champagne tastes much better after midnight, don't you agree?

—*Letter from an Unknown Woman* (1948)

1 sugar cube
2 sprigs fresh peppermint
6 oz. Champagne
1 orange slice

Gently mash the sugar cube and 1 sprig of mint with a muddler (similar to a pestle) in a flute (or a proper silver Julep cup). Fill with Champagne. Gently mix with a bar spoon and garnish with the remaining sprig of peppermint and the orange slice.

Champagne Julep

As served at The Savoy Hotel, London, England

The julep was allegedly invented in Kentucky by Confederate General Albert Sidney Johnson just before the Civil War. It was imported to England in 1840 by the British seaman and novelist Captain Frederick Marryat, who wrote in *A Diary of America, with Remarks on Its Institutions* (1839) that he thought it was one of the "most delightful and insinuating potations [sic] that ever was invented." However, author John Mariani contests this date, stating that the libation was first documented in a book entitled *Travels of Four Years and a Half in the United States of America* (1803) which describes the julep as: "a dram of spirituous liquor that has mint in it, taken by Virginians in the morning."

The julep is the drink that the Governor of Kentucky raises at the Derby's annual Mint Julep toast. It's also the refreshment that Auric Goldfinger offered James Bond in the 1960s thriller, *Goldfinger*. Although most juleps are made with bourbon, brandy, whiskey, or gin, this southern libation can also be created with Champagne.

What's the secret to building a perfect julep? Muddling—using a small wooden muddler (which resembles a pestle) to crush the sugar cube and mint together. Also, never serve a julep with a straw. This drink should be sipped, not slurped. Because—as one aficionado neatly put it—when you're savoring the taste of a perfectly built julep, you can hear the angels sing.

Kir Royale

Some experts say that the kir was developed to unload two of the Burgundy region's less-popular products. The first is a thin, acidy white wine called Aligoté. Unlike its favored cousin—Chardonnay—Aligoté was deemed a second-class citizen until recently. The second is a thick berry liqueur called crème de cassis which was developed in 1841 by Dijonaise businessman Denis Layoute.

Luckily, the name of the sweet-and-dry kir was changed from its original moniker. A popular digestif in neighboring Burgundy around the turn of the century, it was known as *rince cochon* (pig rinse) by the locals. During the 1920s, it was renamed *vin blanc cassis* to differentiate it from another drink called *vermouth cassis*. It was renamed one more time, in 1945, after Felix Kir who was the deputy-mayor of Dijon. Not only was Monsieur Deputy-Mayor the kir's top promoter, he was a member of the French Resistance during the Second World War, a canon of the church, the Dean of Representatives in the French National Assembly, and eventually became the city's mayor until his death in 1968.

The word about kir spread throughout Europe and North America during the 1960s. Soon a number of variations popped up on lounge menus, including the Communiste, Communard, and Cardinale (not to be confused with the gin libation by the same name). But the most famous kir concoction by far is the Kir Royale: a simple blend of crème de cassis and brut Champagne.

4 oz. Champagne
1 oz. crème de cassis
an orange twist

Pour the crème de cassis into a flute. Slowly add the Champagne. Garnish with the orange twist.

The Shrub Royale served
at the Bellagio Resort & Casino in Las Vegas combines
1 splash of each: raspberry shrub (from Tait Farm Foods,
1-800-787-2716) and crème de cassis in a flute with 4
oz. Prosecco, garnished with three fresh raspberries.

The Ritz Hotel in London serves
a Framboise Royale which mixes 1 splash framboise and
5 oz. Champagne in a flute. It also offers The Haugen
which features 1 splash of each: blackberry liqueur and
peach schnappes in a flute. Add 5 oz. Champagne and
garnish with an orange slice.

The Sparkling Berry Splash created
by the Kathy Casey Food Studios in Seattle shakes up
1 splash chambord, 1.5 oz. Smirnoff Black Label vodka,
and 1 oz. raspberry sweet & sour mix in a shaker filled
with ice. Strain into a flute, add 2 oz. Champagne and
garnish with a fresh or frozen raspberry.

A traditional French concoction, the Rue de la Paix
mixes 1 oz. cognac, 2 oz. framboise, and 3 oz.
Champagne in a flute, garnished with a lemon twist.
The classic French Revolution simply replaces
the cognac with brandy.

The Bubble Lounge in New York offers a Ruby Red which
mixes 1 oz. Stoli® Razberi vodka, 1 splash crème de
cassis, and 4 oz. Champagne in a flute.

In his outstanding cookbook, *Dessert Circus* (1998),
Jacques Torres, executive pastry chef at Le Cirque 2000,
offers an innovative twist on the Kir Royale called
Cassis Sticks. Combine 5 oz. water with 3 oz. sugar in a
saucepan. Bring it to a boil. Add 8 oz. whole cassis (black
currants) or fresh blueberries. Stir gently, then pour the
mixture into a loaf pan or other shallow rectangular dish,
so that the mixture is about a half-inch thick. Place it in
the freezer. When it's solid, remove it and cut it into
half-inch rectangles. Then place one cassis stick in
each glass and add Champagne.

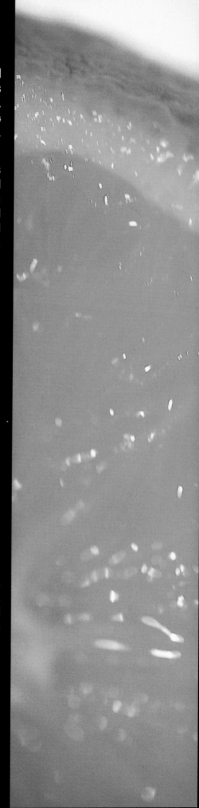

French 75

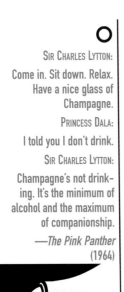

1 tbs. dry gin
1 splash lemon juice
4 oz. Champagne
an orange twist

Pour the gin and lemon juice into a flute. Slowly add the Champagne and garnish with the orange twist.

This drink is named after a 75-millimeter field gun that French forces and the American National Guard used during the First World War. Sipped by officers just before battle, the French 75 cocktail combined effervescent Champagne and aromatic gin (nicknamed "Dutch courage"). While the captains and generals enjoyed this scintillating intoxicant, infantrymen were issued nothing more than a quick shot of blood-warming rum or a glass of pinard (a French colloquialism meaning "raunchy wine").

It's no surprise that this royal cousin to the Martini caught on quickly when the Martini saw its rebirth in modern lounge culture. The resemblance is undeniable, except that the Martini makes its mark with strength while the French 75 does it with its elegance. It's also worth noting that although the French 75 is a bracingly classic concoction, one cannot be too cautious when mixing too many ingredients in the same body on the same night. Pulitzer prize-winning journalist Westbrook Pegler discovered this fact the hard way. He wrote his penance fifty times to fill his daily column in the *New York World Telegram* after a particularly rough night, which read: "I must not mix Champagne, whiskey, and gin. I must not mix Champagne, whiskey, and gin. I must not mix Champagne, whiskey, and gin. . . ."

The teacher I most wanted to emulate, however, was single, drank wine, and had been gassed in World War I. Of his three admirable traits, there was only one I wanted to copy, and sure enough, to this day, I love the sound of a popping cork.

—Russell Baker

Not all Champagne blends are alike. Here's a list of the most popular cuveés:

BLANC DE BLANCS

("White of Whites") are made exclusively with Chardonnay white grapes.

BLANC DE NOIRS

("White of Blacks") are made from Pinot Noir and/or Pinot Meunier black grapes.

ROSÉ CHAMPAGNES

("Pink Champagnes") are produced by either adding red wine to the blend or allowing the pressed juice to remain in contact with the grape skins for a period of time before storage.

CLOS CHAMPAGNES

("Enclosure Champagnes") are made from the grapes grown at only one vineyard. Surprisingly, this is a new style.

The Savoy's French 75 pours 2 oz. dry gin, 1 oz. fresh lemon juice, and 1 tsp. confectioners sugar into a tall, 14 oz. glass filled halfway with cracked ice, then slowly adds 5 oz. Champagne.

An American version called a Champagne Bayou mixes 2 oz. dry gin, 1 tsp. lemon juice, 1 tsp. superfine sugar, and 3 oz. Champagne in a flute.

The I.B.F. Pick-Me-Up served at the Savoy Hotel incorporates 1 ice cube and 3 dashes of each: Fernet Branca and curaçao in a flute. Add 1 oz. brandy and 4 oz. Champagne. Garnish with a lemon twist.

Trader Vic's in Oakland served up The Colonel's Big Opu (the Hawaiian word for "belly") which combines 1 oz. Cointreau, 1 oz. dry gin, 6 oz. Champagne, and the juice from half a lime. Squeeze the lime into a tall, 14 oz. glass and fill halfway with cracked ice. Pour in the gin and Cointreau, then gradually add the Champagne.

The Gerard Lounge in Vancouver serves a Frais de Bois that mixes 1 tbs. strawberry liqueur in a flute with 5 oz. Champagne, garnished with wild strawberries.

The devilish Diabolitan (a contemporary take-off on a Cosmopolitan) mixes 1 splash of each: anisette, strawberry liqueur, and pear liqueur, with 2 oz. dry gin, and 2 oz. Champagne. Pour the liqueurs and gin into a shaker filled with ice. Shake. Strain into a flute, then slowly add the Champagne.

Lola's at Century House serves a Queen Mum which combines 1 oz. dry gin with 4 oz. Champagne in a flute.

A citrusy variation on a Tramonto Sul Garda combines 1 splash Cointreau, 1 splash pink grapefruit juice, 1 oz. dry gin and 4 oz. Champagne in a flute.

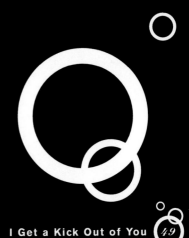

I Get a Kick Out of You

I like Champagne because it tastes like my foot's asleep.
—Art Buchwald

I love Champagne. I think Champagne is very good for the soul and good for your health.
—Robin Leach

CHAPTER 4
57,000,000 *bubbles*
MODERN CHAMPAGNE COCKTAILS

O

In much the same way the folklore surrounding the Martini, the Mint Julep, and single malt scotch is filled with myth and magic, Champagne and Champagne cocktails have a mystique all their own. There are almost as many bits of Champagne lore as there are bubbles in a bottle—44,000,000 to 57,000,000, according to scientific studies.

Tales have been told about the origins of the Champagne coupe and of celebrity baths taken in bubbly. Whole traditions have evolved around Champagne's conspicuous consumption at weddings, the christening of ships, the landing of hot-air balloons, and as the fuel for great romances. Champagne cocktails are the traditional overtures at the annual Vienna Opera Ball, the Cannes Film Festival, the British Open, Wimbledon, treks to Alice Springs in Australia, in the poshest restaurants, lounges, and clubs, as well as on cruise ships around the world.

In our highly practical and unpretentious times, these dazzling libations have even been championed by outrageous characters such as the *Absolutely Fabulous* Edina, her chum Patsy, and that international man of mystery in the movie *Austin Powers*.

Marie Antoinette

As served at The Ritz Hotel, London, England

From Madames Clicquot and Bollinger to Marie Antoinette and Maria Federovna, women have contributed greatly to Champagne folklore. Besides being the wife of France's King Louis XVI, Josephe Jeanne Marie Antoinette was the center of much political opposition and gossip during her reign as that nation's queen. She ultimately—and literally—lost her head at the age of thirty-eight during the French Revolution. As the story goes, it was due to her last, smug remark. When told the peasants had no bread to eat, the queen commented: "Let them eat cake."

Marie's problems began right after her coronation at the age of nineteen, when word leaked out onto the Paris streets that her majesty was extravagant, trashing conventions as well the treasury to appease her desire for outrageous breast-revealing clothes, diamond necklaces, and fine foods.

Despite her infamy, Marie Antoinette left two legacies that are unique to Champagne lore. Her name graces a cocktail served at London's Ritz Hotel and the shape of her breast allegedly served as the model for the saucer-shaped glass—called a coupe—which was highly fashionable from the 1890s to the 1940s.

[Champagne] has the taste of an apple peeled with a steel knife.

—Aldous Huxley commenting on the taste of a bottle of 1916 Roederer

You know my way with the women; Champagne's the thing; make 'em drink, make 'em talk...make 'em do anything.

—William Makepeace Thackeray (1840)

1 splash of each: strawberry liqueur, Cointreau, calvados, and fresh lemon juice
4 oz. Champagne

Combine strawberry liqueur, Cointreau, calvados, and juice in a shaker filled with ice. Strain into a flute and slowly add Champagne.

According to author Hugh Johnson, Marie commissioned the Sèvres porcelain factory to take a cast of her breast and to produce four white coupes. Each cast was to be mounted on a base of three porcelain goat's heads. The coupes themselves were used to adorn her majesty's Dairy Temple at the Château de Rambouillet near Versailles. (Somehow it's hard to picture a modern-day First Lady making a request like that.)

Even though author John Doxat insinuated in his *Booth's Handbook of Cocktails and Mixed Drinks* (1966) that the coupe was a British invention developed "so chorus girls of the [eighteen] nineties would not hiccup on too much effervescence in their bubbly," we prefer to err on the side of Marie Antoinette. There's still one of her "size-A" coupes on display at Château de Rambouillet.

The Bellagio Cocktail served at the Bellagio Resort & Casino in Las Vegas combines 4 oz. Roatari Italian Sparkling Wine, 1 oz. Alize Red Passion, and 1 oz. French passion fruit coulis in a flute.

The Ritz also mixes up a Gloria using 1 splash of each: strawberry liqueur, lychee liqueur, dry vermouth, and lemon juice in a shaker filled with ice. Strain into a flute and add 4 oz. Champagne.

The Bubble Lounge's Fraise is a purist's dream. Three small whole fresh strawberries are served in a flute filled with 4 oz. rosé Champagne.

Lola's at Century House serves the Big Apple which mixes 1 oz. calvados and 4 oz. Champagne in a flute.

The Ritz Hotel in London makes a Nightliner that combines 1 splash of each: apricot brandy, calvados, orange juice, and lemon juice in a shaker filled with ice. Strain into a flute and add 4 oz. Champagne.

The Red Ambrosia mixes 1 dash strawberry liqueur, 2 oz. Hawaiian Punch, and 3 oz. Champagne in a flute.

The ubiquitous I.B.U. blends 1 splash brandy, 1 splash apricot brandy, and 1 oz. fresh orange juice with 4 oz. Champagne in a flute.

Champagne Bath

There have been times in the course of romance when the only proper way to drink Champagne was out of your lover's shoe. We didn't uncover much evidence to support this variation on a foot fetish (we don't recommend it; even good leather does nothing for the taste of Champagne). However, we did learn that Champagne baths have had generations of celebrated fans. Almost since Champagne's birth, rumors have flown about people luxuriating in Champagne baths: from historical figures like Catherine the Great to more modern celebrities such as Marilyn Monroe (who once used 350 bottles for a Champagne bath) and Dennis Hopper (who was allegedly accompanied by Natalie Wood).

Broadway producer Florenz Ziegfeld's estranged wife—the French musical and screen star Anna Held—was one of the celebrity residents at San Francisco's St. Francis Hotel who gained an outrageous reputation. Before she had even crossed the Atlantic to win the hearts of American theatergoers, Miss Held became famous for taking milk baths. This fetish required thirty gallons of pasteurized milk to be delivered to her hotel suite daily. But she once confessed that she preferred something more bubbly. "The milk baths are for publicity,"

God only made water, but man made wine.
—Victor Hugo

How ironic that Champagne—long associated with sin and luxury—should have been invented by a blind monk!
—Randolph Fillmore

1 dash Cherry Herring liqueur
1 or 2 drops rose water
5 oz. Champagne
a brandied cherry
3 rose petals

Place the rose petals and cherry in a flute. Add the liqueur and rose water, then slowly pour the Champagne on top.

she purred. "Champagne is strictly reserved for pleasure." A similar sentiment was voiced in more recent times by a "Page-Three Girl" for London's *Sun* named Katie and her male counterpart Rhydian Lewis. They had been hired by the notorious London tabloid to dip into a bathtub filled with thirty-six bottles of bubbly at the Portobello Hotel. It was the same place and same room in which supermodel Kate Moss and actor Johnny Depp were rumored to have tried it, using £750 worth of Champagne. Unlike Miss Moss (who refused to comment on the matter) the buxom young Katie remarked to reporters: "It's chilly, but oh so sexy. The bubbles seem to get everywhere—and I mean everywhere!"

There are also Champagne rituals you can enjoy with your clothes on. We discovered one quite by accident while we were dining in a tiny bistro in Vancouver's West End, Chez Thierry. We had ordered a bottle of Champagne as the accompaniment to our *maigret*

(duck breast) in a fresh peach and port sauce. The affable owner who had taken our order, Thierry Damilano, nodded with approval, disappearing into the back. He popped out a few minutes later wearing a Napoleonic uniform complete with hat. In one hand, he had our unopened Champagne bottle and in the other, a cutlass. That's right—a sword. Before we had a chance to say "Don't worry, we'll pay our check," he cleaved off the cork and the top of the bottle with a clean, angled sweep of his

cutlass, and he began pouring the frothy liquid into our awaiting flutes.

After much slightly nervous applause from us—as well as the restaurant's other patrons—we discovered that Thierry is a member of the esteemed Confrèrie du Sabre d'Or, a French brotherhood dedicated to the art of cork sabering. (He's also the former coach of the Canadian national women's wind surfing team and a master yachtsman.)

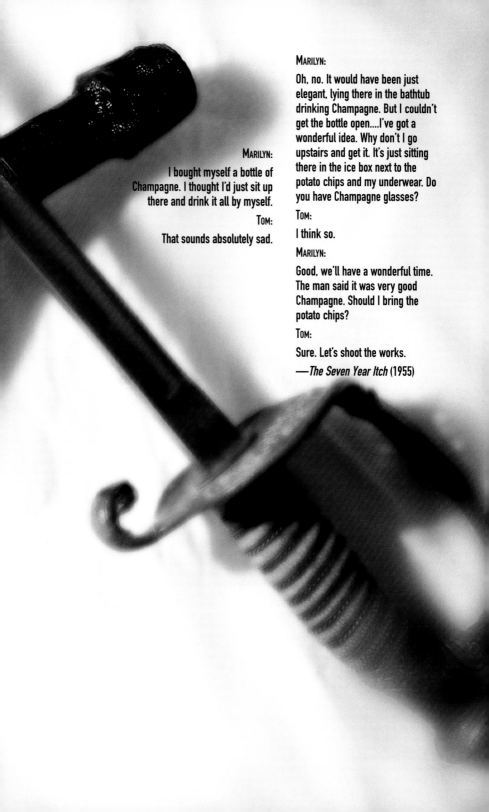

MARILYN:

I bought myself a bottle of Champagne. I thought I'd just sit up there and drink it all by myself.

TOM:

That sounds absolutely sad.

MARILYN:

Oh, no. It would have been just elegant, lying there in the bathtub drinking Champagne. But I couldn't get the bottle open....I've got a wonderful idea. Why don't I go upstairs and get it. It's just sitting there in the ice box next to the potato chips and my underwear. Do you have Champagne glasses?

TOM:

I think so.

MARILYN:

Good, we'll have a wonderful time. The man said it was very good Champagne. Should I bring the potato chips?

TOM:

Sure. Let's shoot the works.

—*The Seven Year Itch* (1955)

He explained that he'd sabered hundreds of corks off Champagne bottles over the years, pointing to the shelves lined with corks—still collared with the glass necks that had snapped cleanly off.

There are six steps to sabering a Champagne bottle, according to the Confrèrie du Sabre d'Or:

1. The Champagne has to be thoroughly chilled and kept still for at least forty-eight hours. This ensures that viewers won't be showered with too much of the contents.

2. Remove the foil that covers the cork and the neck of the bottle.

3. Delicately remove the *muselet* (wire cage) from the cork.

4. Locate the seam of the bottle with your fingertips.

5. Remove any foil that conceals the seam along the entire length of the bottle.

6. Hold the bottle firmly, with your arm extended and the neck pointing up. Without using force, slide the flat of the saber along the seam until it hits the lip at the top of the neck. Follow through with the arm movement. The neck should break off cleanly with the cork in place.

The actual act of lopping off the cork takes a great deal of practice, confidence, and subtlety. Only a handful of people in Canada and the United States have been conferred with a Diplome de Sabreur from the brotherhood.

MACAULAY CONNOR:

I bring you greetings. Cinderella's slipper. It's called Champagne. Champagne is the great leveller.

—*The Philadelphia Story* (1940)

But Thierry is not the only saber master we've witnessed in action. A year later, we were present at the induction of a new member to the brotherhood. After sabering a bottle which was then poured onto a ten-foot tall Champagne fountain built out of coupes, Charles Woo (owner of the Sutton Place Hotel chain) was presented with his diploma at a lavish ceremony held in the ballroom of the Vancouver Sutton Place Hotel.

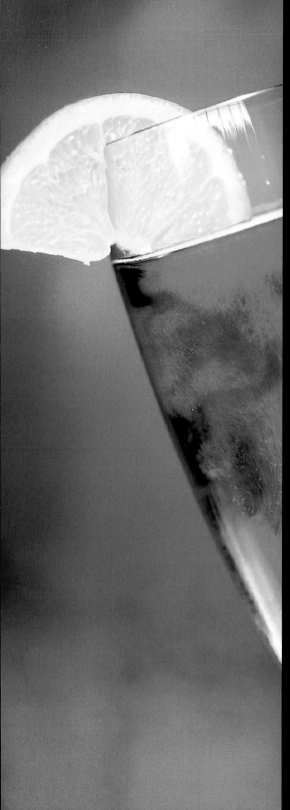

Matthew's in Manhattan serves a
Love Potion #10 which mixes up
1 scoop of rose gernamium sorbet
(combining rose geranium petals, dry
muscat wine, and sugar) with 5 oz.
rosé Champagne, garnished with
fresh rose petals.

A party-sized Empire City Punch
combines 1 pint fresh strawberries,
2 liters sparkling mineral water, 4 oz.
maraschino liqueur, 4 oz. curaçao,
4 oz. Benedictine, 1 oz. dark rum,
1 bottle brandy, 6 bottles Champagne,
4 bottles tokay wine, 2 bottles
madeira wine, and 4 bottles margaux
wine in a huge punch bowl. Serve on
a bed of crushed ice and decorate
with orange, pineapple, and lemon
slices.

The Southern Lady served at the
Cedar Grove Plantation in Edgefield,
South Carolina, mixes 1 tsp. Cherry
Marnier liqueur with 5 oz.
Champagne in a flute, garnished with
a stemmed cherry and 3 rose petals.

Lola's at Century House serves a
Maiden Marion which mixes up 1 oz.
cherry brandy with 4 oz. Champagne,
garnished with a maraschino cherry.

The Ritz Hotel in London mixes
up a Pink Passion by pouring
1 splash of each: vodka, cherry
brandy, crème de cassis, and grapefruit juice into a flute, followed by
4 oz. Champagne.

The Southern Belle combines
1 tbs. amaretto, 1 tbs. apricot brandy,
and 4. oz. Champagne in a flute.

The Ritz Hotel in London serves a Pimms Royale which combines 1 splash Pimms No. 1 with 5 oz. Champagne in a flute.

Absolutely Fabulous

As served at Lola's at Century House, Vancouver, Canada

Style consciousness never really died despite the death of yuppiedom, the rise of Gen-X, and the nesting of the thirty-somethings, which all seemed to happen during the 1990s. It's just that some old traditions have become seriously fashionable again. Take Martini-drinking and swing music, for example. There's those of us who remember that our parents liked all that stuff—not us cooler-than-cool youth who drifted on Tequila Sunrises and Strawberry Daiquiris back in the disco seventies. In London, hip and stylish have been more than states of mind since the sixties for rebellious, affluent souls who have defied repressive convention since birth. Look at the ex-Sloane Ranger types that starred in the Jennifer Saunders/Dawn French BBC hit *Absolutely Fabulous*.

Neither Patsy the fashion editor nor Edina the PR maven would have touched a bottle of gin with a stuffy name like Pimms No. 1 (let alone a cocktail called an Absolutely Fabulous or a Pimms Royale) back in the swinging sixties. I mean, it was all sex and drugs and rock and roll washed down with cheap wine, wasn't it, darling?

A nicely-balanced meal, preceded by a couple of dry Martinis, washed down with half a bot.
—P.G. Wodehouse
Very Good, Jeeves! (1930)

Wine is one of the few remaining luxury items worth paying too much for.
—Herb Caen

1 splash Pimms No. 1 (a flavored dry gin)
5 oz. Champagne
a cucumber slice

Pour the Pimms into a flute and gradually add the Champagne. Garnish with the cucumber slice.

Nelson's Blood

One of the British navy's greatest heroes was Viscount Horatio Nelson, who guarded his nation's interests in the Caribbean, Egypt, and the Mediterranean during the late eighteenth century. He received the greatest honor of all in the early twentieth century when his name was given to a popular cocktail that combines two favorite British beverages: Champagne and port.

1 oz. ruby or vintage port

4 oz. Champagne

Frost the rim with sugar (see page 22). Pour in the port, then gradually add the Champagne

Back in the days of the berserk Vikings, ships were christened in a rather macabre fashion: a selected victim was sacrificed on each new vessel's prow to ensure that his departed spirit would be compelled to guard the craft on its raids along the North Sea. These ethereal figureheads cost lives in a land with a relatively small population. Consequently, wiser heads prevailed. Red wine replaced the traditional blood. This civilized modification ensured the continuation of the Viking blood line, coincided with concepts preached by visiting Christian missionaries, and seemed to adequately appease the ancient Norse gods that ruled the cruel and unpredictable seas.

The practice of christening a new frigate or galleon with wine spread in time to other seafaring nations such as Great Britain, Spain, and France. (Although the ancient Greeks were spilling wine all over their decks way before it became fashionable.)

Around the mid-1700s, the French made one more adjustment to this seafaring tradition: shipbuilders christened their new vessels with bottles of Champagne. As it was a wish for safe passage, they undoubtedly figured they'd better use the best wine they could. Others soon followed suit, and the tradition has remained intact to this day.

Champagne Cocktails

O

Deep in the Baltic Sea off the Finnish coast, a two-masted, 82-foot schooner, the *Jonkoping*, lay in its 210-foot deep, watery grave. It had been sent to the bottom by a German submarine on November 3, 1916. Bound for pre-revolutionary Russia, the schooner's cargo included 5,000 bottles of 1907 Heidsieck Monopole Champagne, 9,500 gallons of cognac, and 1,600 gallons of red wine for the members of the czarist Russian court and army. In May 1998, a team of Swedish divers exhumed 2,000 bottles of Champagne that had been perfectly preserved in the dark, 35°F (4°C) waters. Despite being submerged for decades, they were still quite bubbly, and deemed delicious by experts. Twenty-four of these bottles were auctioned at Christie's in September of that year, fetching more than £500 per bottle. Despite the international fanfare and celebration at their discovery, when French wine experts asked the year of the Champagne found in the hold, the divers replied, "1907." There was a pause and sigh: "What a shame," the experts reputedly replied, "1907. That really was a rather disappointing year."

The White's Club mixes 1 oz. tawny port with 4 oz. Champagne in a flute. Frost the rim (see page 22) with port and sugar before pouring or garnish with a lemon twist.

A Cold Duck recipe mixes 2 oz. red Bordeaux wine with 3 oz. Champagne. Other versions use moselle wine and a pinch of sugar to sweeten the finish.

A Lillet Chelsea Feast recipe mixes 2 oz. Lillet Rouge and 1 dash ginger ale with 3 oz. Champagne.

The Griffin served at the Tuscarora Mill in Leesburg, Virginia adds 4 oz. Champagne to 1 oz. Pineau des Charentes (a fortified red wine similar to port) in a flute. This same libation is called a Bacchus at Lola's at Century House, where it's garnished with frozen grapes.

Lola's at Century House offers a La Vie en Rose. Put 2 drops rose water onto a sugar cube and place in a flute. Add 5 oz. Champagne and garnish with a fresh rose petal.

The Melony served at Lola's mixes 1 oz. melon liqueur with 4 oz. Champagne in a flute.

The Prince William at Lola's combines 1 splash pear liqueur with 5 oz. Champagne in a flute.

A Monte Carlo mixes 2 oz. dry gin, 1 splash crème de menthe, and 1 splash lemon juice with 3 oz. Champagne in a flute.

An Arise My Love simply combines 1 splash white crème de menthe and 5 oz. Champagne in a flute. Frost the rim of the flute with green creme de menthe and sugar (see page 22).

The Hemingway is served in eastern Europe, adding 1 splash Pernod (an anise-flavored liqueur) to 5 oz. Champagne in a flute.

The Sirius Stargarita served at Pops for Champagne in Chicago combines 1 oz. tequila with 4 oz. Champagne, garnished with a lime twist.

At Johnny Cairo's Bar & Grill in Puerto Morelos, Mexico, the Champagne Margarita serves up 1 oz. tequila and 1 splash of each: Cointreau, lime juice, and orange juice. Add 4 oz. Champagne in a flute. Frost the rim of the flute with raw sugar and Cointreau (see page 22) and garnish with a lime twist.

The best story we've ever heard about christening a craft occurred when Moët et Chandon's American sales agent, George Kessler, substituted a bottle of Champagne for the customary bottle of *sekt* (a German sparkling wine) at the launching of Kaiser Wilhelm II's yacht—the *Meteor III*—in San Francisco Bay. Kessler's publicity stunt was not taken well by his royal highness. Wilhelm—who was the emperor of both Germany and Prussia—hastily recalled his ambassador.

At one time [Mark Twain's] drinking got all mixed up with his health fads, and he got it into his head that he needed hot Scotch or Champagne or ale or beer—the formula varied from time to time—to put him to sleep.

—An anonymous
Mark Twain biographer

MACAULAY CONNOR:

Champagne's funny stuff. I'm used to whiskey. Whiskey is a slap on the back, and Champagne's a heavy mist before my eyes.
—*The Philadelphia Story* (1940)

TINTIN:

Great snakes! Tins of crab!...Champagne, too! Snowy, my boy, our supplies are taken care of.

SNOWY:

And how!
—Hergé,
The Crab with the Golden Claws (1953)

Americana

Viking Eric the Red dubbed North America "Vineland" when he arrived in the tenth century, and his son, Leif Erikson, called it by the same name. Little did they know that it would someday reflect America's love affair with sparkling wines. Our founding fathers, including George Washington, toasted the birth of the nation in 1776 with glasses of Champagne. (According to one rumor, Champagne was Martha Washington's favorite drink—and George kept a liberal supply on hand to keep her happy.) Alongside smooth Tennessee whiskey and Kentucky bourbon, Champagne poured like water from coast to coast. The Americana cocktail tips its hat to the marriage of smoky, sweet bourbon and light, effervescent Champagne.

According to the authors of *Champagne!*, Isaac Cronin and Rafael Pallais, the luckiest prospectors that flooded San Francisco's hotels and saloons after striking rich along the American River in 1849 were known to wash the gold dust (and six months' worth of dirt) off their bodies in bathtubs filled with frothy Champagne.

In the aftermath of the San Francisco earthquake of 1906, survivors of this catastrophe drowned their sorrows and rejoiced in being alive by purchasing more than a railcar load of Champagne.

1 tsp. bourbon
1 dash Angostura bitters
5 oz. Champagne
fresh peach slice

Pour the bourbon and bitters into a flute. Then slowly add the Champagne and garnish

The Crystal Peach mixes 1 oz. bourbon and 1 dash Fee Bros. peach bitters with 4 oz. Champagne in a flute.

The Kathy Casey Food Studios makes a Rusty Champagne Cocktail that mixes 1 dash of each: Drambouie and Oban scotch in a flute. Slowly add 5 oz. Champagne

Champagne itself would never have survived without good old American resourcefulness. Four years later, in 1910, when the root-killing *phylloxera vastatrix* louse threatened to decimate the Champagne region's precious vineyards (as it had done to grape crops throughout Europe), Americans came to the rescue. It was discovered that the louse-resistant roots of Californian vines could be grafted to the indigenous Champenois Chardonnay, Pinot Noir and Pinot Meunier vines, protecting the delicate source of the world's favorite wine.

America came to Champagne's rescue again during the Second World War when Gen. George S. Patton liberated the city of Épernay in the Champagne region on August 28, 1944. Luckily, local producers had managed to conceal more than enough Champagne to celebrate their freedom with the GIs, despite the fact they had been forced to ship 400,000 bottles per week to Adolf Hitler and his staff. In possibly the best indication that the war was favoring the Allies, one Nazi aide observed that Champagne was not served at the Fuehrer's fiftieth birthday celebration on April 20, 1945: "It is only that day that I knew we had lost the war."

Sputnik

As served at the Bubble Lounge, New York, NY

Since its beginnings Champagne has been part of the courting process. It's a way to make a great impression, showing flair and taste. It's no different with sparkling cocktails like the Sputnik, which blends the best of both French and Russian flavors into a perfect match. No, the name doesn't imply that its consumption will send you into orbit. Sputnik (it means loosely, "partner in life") is a Russian colloquialism that suggests romance and wooing.

Most successful suitors around the world will agree, the way to a woman's heart is to shower her with flowers, chocolates, and Champagne. Remember when that international man of mystery Austin Powers set about wooing his partner Vanessa Kensington by taking her for a night on the town, including a Champagne dinner atop a double-decker bus followed by a game of Twister in their hotel suite? That's romance mod style, baby. The other British superspy, James Bond, offered more than one female companion a little Champagne to wash down anything from a plate of Makaroff caviar in a Monte Carlo casino to sandwiches procured from the club car on a train bound for Kentucky.

VANESSA:
Austin, come have some Champagne with me.
AUSTIN [flopping onto the bed]:
Oh, I tripped.
—*Austin Powers: International Man of Mystery* (1997)

According to urban legend, you are more likely to be killed by a Champagne cork than by a black widow spider.

1 oz. Stolichnaya Ohranj Vodka
1 oz. fresh orange juice
1 splash grenadine syrup
3 oz. Champagne

Frost the rim of a flute with sugar in the raw and grenadine syrup (see page 22). Add the vodka, juice, and grenadine syrup, then pour in the Champagne.

The chocolate vodka we mention in some of our recipes is called Goldenbärr. It's new to the States and it's the only one on the market. So if it's not available in your area yet, ask for it. We were amazed when a friend sent us a bottle from New York. Underlying the essence of chocolate is a truly top-notch, classic Ukrainian vodka. Unlike crème de cacao and chocolate liqueurs, Goldenbärr is not sugary, lending drinks a remarkably clear, pure flavor.

Champagne, if you are seeking the truth, is better than a lie detector. It encourages a man to be expansive, even reckless, while lie detectors are only a challenge to tell lies successfully.

—Graham Greene, *Travels with My Aunt* (1969)

The Métro combines 1 splash cranberry juice, 1 dash Rose's lime juice, 1 dash Cointreau, and 1 oz. vodka, with 4 oz. Champagne in a flute.

A Poinsettia combines 1 oz. cranberry juice and 4 oz. Champagne, garnished with an orange wedge.

The Bubble Lounge's Mimi "Bubble" Zaza combines 1 splash of each: Cointreau, vodka, and orange juice. Add 4 oz. Champagne; garnish with an orange twist.

The Bubble Lounge's Caribbean Contessa mixes 1 splash of each: Cointreau, cranberry juice, orange juice, and vodka. Add 4 oz. Champagne in a flute.

Lola's at Century House offers a Blue Velvet that marries 1 splash blue curaçao and 5 oz. Champagne in a flute.

The Palm Court mixes 2 oz. fresh orange juice, 1 oz. Grand Marnier, 1 dash Fee Bros. peach bitters, and 2 oz. Champagne in a flute.

Pops for Champagne in Chicago serves a Celestial Fizz which combines 1 oz. cognac, 1 tbs. Grand Marnier, 2 oz. cranberry juice, and 2 oz. Champagne in a flute, garnished with a lemon twist.

The Ritz Hotel's Fizz combines 1 splash of each: amaretto, blue curaçao, and lemon juice with 4 oz. Champagne in a flute.

Lola's at Century House also makes a Lynette which combines 1 splash Grand Marnier with 5 oz. Champagne in a flute topped with a fresh strawberry.

The Chicago is made by mixing 1 oz. brandy, 1 dash curaçao, and 2 dashes Angostura bitters, with 4 oz. Champagne. Frost the rim of the flute with lemon juice and sugar before pouring (see page 22).

Pops for Champagne in Chicago makes a Citrus Centauri which blends 1.5 oz. lemon-flavored vodka, 1 splash Rose's lime juice, and 1 splash blue curaçao with 3 oz. Champagne. Garnish with a lemon twist.

The Golden Kiss mixes 1 oz. Goldenbärr Chocolate Vodka with 4 oz. Champagne in a flute. One variation, called a Golden Passion, adds 1 splash Alize passion fruit liqueur to the mix.

Du Monde

Based on the signature cocktail served
at Piccolo Mondo, Vancouver, Canada

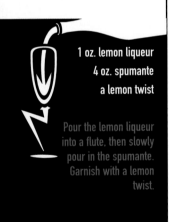

1 oz. lemon liqueur
4 oz. spumante
a lemon twist

Pour the lemon liqueur
into a flute, then slowly
pour in the spumante.
Garnish with a lemon
twist.

The uplifting, citrus character found in the Du Monde (literally, "of the world") reminds us of the daring protagonist in Jules Verne's novel *Around the World in Eighty Days* (1873), Phileas T. Fogg. He wagered that he could circumnavigate the world in a hot-air balloon. Probably due to the number of stops he made, this wily Londoner dispensed with one custom commonly associated with balloon flight: the presentation of a bottle of Champagne upon each landing. It's a tradition that began at the conclusion of an event that changed the world.

On November 21, 1783, the first manned flight in a free-floating balloon took place. Inventors Joseph and Jacques Montgolfier had already demonstrated the unpiloted capability of their hot-air balloon with a ten-minute flight over Annonay, France, on June 5, 1783.

Their project sparked the interest of King Louis XVI and his queen, Marie Antoinette, who granted the Montgolfiers' request to perform a manned-flight demonstration. Two gentlemen of the royal court—Jean Pilatre de Rozier and the Marquis d'Arlandes—thought it would garner some personal notoriety in

The Bubble Lounge's Tropical Demoiselle mixes 1 splash of each: passion fruit juice, orange juice, and pineapple juice. Add 4 oz. Champagne in a flute.

A variation on a classic Boom Boom Punch mixes 1 oz. dark rum, 1 tbs. orange juice, 1 oz. sweet vermouth, and 3 oz. Champagne in a flute, garnished with banana slices.

The Ocho Rios combines 1 splash white rum, 1 splash banana liqueur, and 2 dashes Fee Bros. orange bitters with 4 oz. Champagne, garnished with a banana slice.

The Tibetan Monkey served at Lola's at Century House combines 1 splash banana liqueur with 5 oz. Champagne in a flute.

Oliver's in Seattle serves a Kumquat Cocktail that mixes 1 splash kumquat nectar with 5 oz. Champagne in a flute, garnished with a lemon twist and a marinated kumquat.

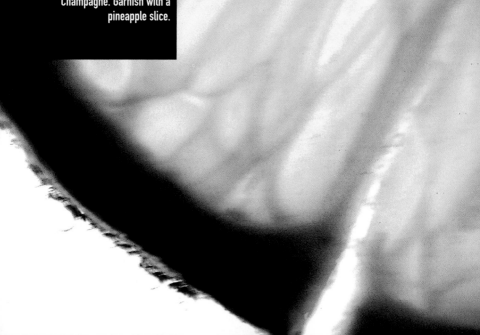

An American Flyer mixes 1 oz. white rum, 1 tsp. fresh lime juice, and 1 sugar cube, with 4 oz. Champagne in a flute, garnished with a lime slice.

A variation on this theme —the Airmail—replaces the sugar cube with 1 tsp. honey.

The China Clipper mixes 1 oz. dry gin, 1 oz. white rum, 1 splash Rose's Lime Juice, 1 splash lemon juice, and 3 oz. Champagne in a flute, garnished with a lemon twist.

The Keuka Cup concocts 1 splash lemon juice with 4 oz. Champagne in a flute, garnished with pineapple chunks and an orange slice.

A Clair de Lune combines 1 tbs. crème de menthe, 1 tbs. pineapple juice, 1 oz. dry gin, and 2 drops curaçao into a shaker filled with ice. Strain into a flute and add 3 oz. Champagne. Garnish with a pineapple slice.

the history books if they volunteered to fly. They got their wish.

The Montgolfier brothers' paper-and-silk balloon elevated the noblemen five hundred feet above the center of Paris, conveying them over rooftops and past cathedrals for twenty-two minutes before landing in the vineyards of northern France. (We're not sure if they landed in the Champagne region, but it would be nice to conjecture.)

No one had ever witnessed such a feat—especially not the local growers. On seeing the two men descending from the sky in a basket, there was a scream to the effect of: "They must be devils!" Luckily, pilots Rozier and d'Arlandes had the perfect peace offering on hand: bottles of Champagne.

We discovered that this custom is not about to fade into obscurity when we attended the launch of seventy-four hot-air balloons at 6 AM along the Boise River. The modern-day balloon-ists participating in this three-day rally, an annual event, arrive with their crews in droves. One vehicle had a bumper sticker that read: "Champagne and Propane: Breakfast of Balloonists."

Many balloons conveyed more than just the pilot, carrying passengers who had booked a spot in the basket months in advance. Along with startled landowners, passengers are frequently offered a post-flight libation. (One Scottish balloon-ing company entices potential passengers for their one-hour flights by adding in their brochure: "Once landed, the crew, who have been following by road under instruction of the pilot to collect us, will help to pack the balloon away and then offer you a glass of Champagne or Buck's Fizz....")

Most ground crews are manned by a spouse or a close relative who is as addicted to this unique sport as the pilot, but there are freelancers as well. On the final day of this particular rally, we spotted a female crew member wearing an embroi-dered jacket that professed her sentiments: "We crew for Champagne."

1 oz. cognac
4 oz. Champagne

Pour cognac into a flute, then slowly add the Champagne.

Imperial Duo

As served at The Bubble Lounge, San Francisco, CA

Nearly every engaged couple dreams of having the perfect wedding ceremony: a day to remember happily for the rest of their lives. The modern world has had more than a few fairy tale marriages, uniting some very familiar royal couples, whom we toast with an Imperial Duo.

In 1947, Princess Elizabeth Alexandra Mary married Prince Philip on national television six years before she was crowned queen of England. In 1956, the marriage of film star Grace Kelly to Prince Rainier Louis Henri Maxence Bertrand de Grimaldi of Monaco was like a page lifted from every young girl's dream of wedding a handsome—and fabulously rich—prince. An American student named Hope Cook married Palden Thondup Namgyal, the last hereditary king of the Himalayan country, Sikkim, during the early 1960s. And the "wedding of the century" was, of course, the 1981 internationally-televised union between England's crown Prince of Wales—Charles—and Lady Diana Frances, daughter of the eighth Earl of Spencer.

The truth is, during the ceremony and the reception, every bridal couple gets a taste of what it's like to be royalty (and anyone who's been a bride or groom might wonder how royalty survives being the center of attention at years of weekly—even daily—gala events). After the nerve-wracking walk down the aisle and other ceremonies, the ubiquitous Champagne toast marks a truly joyous end of the formalities and the beginning of the festivities.

The King's Peg blends 1 oz. brandy with 4 oz. Champagne in a flute. The Queen's Peg mixes 1 oz. dry gin with 4 oz. Champagne.

The Schussboomer's Delight mixes 1 oz. cognac and 1 tbs. fresh lemon juice with 4 oz. Champagne in a flute.

A Luxury Cocktail blends 2 oz. brandy and 2 dashes Fee Bros. orange bitters with 3 oz. Champagne in a flute.

The dashing Prince of Wales blends 1 oz. madeira wine, 1 oz. brandy, 1 dash curaçao, 1 dash Angostura bitters, and 3 oz. Champagne in a flute.

The Velvet Swing blends 1 splash armagnac and 2 oz. ruby port with 3 oz. Champagne in a flute. Optionally, this can be garnished with small, fresh rose petals.

Pops for Champagne in Chicago offers a Betelgeuse which blends 1 oz. Stoli® Vanil Vodka, 1 tbs. vanilla liqueur, 1 tbs. Rose's Lime Juice, and 1 oz. white zinfandel wine with 2 oz. Champagne in a flute.

Here's how to say "Happy New Year" in a few different places around the world:

AUSTRIA

Glückliches neues jahr!

BELGIUM

Gelukkig nieuwjaar!

BRAZIL

Feliz ano novo!

CHINA

Gung hai fat choy!

CZECH REPUBLIC

Stastny Novy Rok!

DENMARK

Godt nytaar!

FRANCE

Bonne année!

GERMANY

Prosit neujahr!

ISRAEL

L'shanah tovah tikatevu!

ITALY

Felice anno nuovo!

JAPAN

Akemashite omedetou gozaimasu!

MEXICO/SPAIN

Feliz año nuevo!

THE NETHERLANDS

Zalig nieuwjaar!

SCOTLAND

Au gui l'an neuf!

THAILAND

Kwam suk pee mai!

Moulin Rouge

Born in France, the Moulin Rouge cocktail is the grande dame ancestor to a modern-day libation that's appreciated by tragically hip Londoners like *Ab Fab* characters Edina and Patsy. However, their brand-conscious natures dictated that they nickname it "Bolly-Stolly" for the top-shelf ingredients—Bollinger and Stolichnaya—used in their version of the recipe.

The romance between Russia and France has a long and passionate history. It began when Czar Peter the Great had his agent place an order for *Champagne mousseux* shortly after he decreed on December 20, 1699, that January First—Christian New Year's Day—would be celebrated throughout the Russian empire, despite the objections raised by his Judaic, Islamic, Buddhist, and pagan subjects. The relationship deepened when Madame Clicquot smuggled casks of her vintage 1811 Comet rosé Champagne to Czarina Maria Feodorovna—wife of Czar Alexander I—who wanted a special drink to celebrate her husband's return from the battlefront (and despite Napoleon Bonaparte's embargo on exports to eastern Europe). This tête-a-tête continued when royal refugees from Czar Nicholas II's court toasted their escape from the ravages of the Russian Revolution in 1917 by fleeing to Paris—their emotional home away from home—and consuming large quantities of Champagne.

However, the turn of a new year is still one of the best reasons to eat, drink, and be merry. One of the oldest documented New Year's fests in the western hemisphere took place in Babylon around 2000 BC. Honoring the chief god, Marduk, the feast was held during the spring equinox (March 20 or 21), which people of the time believed marked the annual

1 oz. vodka
4 oz. Champagne

Pour the vodka into a flute. Then slowly pour in the Champagne. Garnish with an orange twist if desired.

transition of time itself. They also started the tradition of making resolutions about their behavior and actions during the next year (though party hats and horns came much later).

Blame Roman emperor Julius Caesar for establishing New Year's Day on January first around 46 BC. In keeping with his deified ego, the emperor devised his own calendar, dedicating each month to a specific god. He chose the gatekeeper of heaven and hell—Janus—as the guardian of the Julian calendar's first month. He even dictated that all Romans should celebrate before the temple of Janus on the first day of his new, improved Julian year.

Not everyone celebrates the turn of the calendrical cycle on January first despite Julius Caesar's attempts to unite the entire world under Roman rule. The Judaic calendar continues to view Tishri (the seventh lunar month after the spring equinox) as the start of the new year. In many parts of India, the populace just can't get enough of New Year's festivities, celebrating *varusha pirappu* (the birth of the New Year) on April 14 and *diwali* (a festival of lights dedicated to Lakshimi, the goddess of wealth and prosperity) during the tenth lunar month. Since 1699, the Sikhs of the north Punjab have celebrated the birth of their sect on April 14, by taking a ceremonial "new year" bath before sunrise. The Chinese continue to commemorate their New Year on the second new moon after the winter solstice (December 22), just as they have for over five thousand years.

It doesn't really matter where you spend New Year's Eve or with how many people, just as long as you know how to celebrate it. Put on your party clothes (there's no such thing as being overdressed on New Year's Eve), pour yourself a Champagne cocktail, and salute the end of the old year while you welcome in the new.

The Absolutely Fabulous version—Bolly-Stolly—is simple, but delicious. Pour 1 oz. Stolichnaya vodka in a flute, then gradually add 4 oz. Bollinger Champagne.

A Vodka Champagne Punch combines 1 oz. vodka, 1 tbs. white rum, 1 tsp. fresh lime juice, and 1 tsp. strawberry liqueur with 3 oz. Champagne in a flute. Frost the rim of the flute with pink decorating sugar and strawberry liqueur (see page 22) and garnish with a fresh strawberry.

The Eiffel View combines 1 oz. citrus vodka, 1 splash grenadine syrup, 4 oz. Champagne in a flute. The Mandarin Cocktail mixes 1 oz. orange-flavored vodka with 4 oz. Champagne in a flute.

Asia de Cuba in New York serves a Mambo King that combines 1 oz. Stoli® Razberi vodka with 4 oz. Champagne. Frost the rim with grenadine syrup and raw sugar (see page 22).

The Raspberry Truffle combines 1 oz. Stoli® Razberi Vodka and 1 splash Godiva Chocolate Liqueur with 4 oz. Champagne in a flute.

The Panacea served at Oliver's in Seattle pours 1 tbs. crème de cassis in an ice-cold shaker. Swirl to coat and pour out about half. Fill halfway with ice, then add 1 oz. Finlandia Cranberry vodka, 1 tbs. fresh lime juice (sweetened to taste), and 1 splash Cointreau. Shake and strain into a flute. Add 3 oz. Champagne and garnish with a whole cranberry and a lime twist.

The Martini Royale combines 3 oz. vodka or dry gin with 1 oz. Champagne in a Martini glass (stirred gently), garnished with a lemon twist.

Oliver's in Seattle serves a French Kiss that mixes 1 oz. vodka and 1 tbs. Lillet Blanc with 3 oz. Champagne, garnished with an orange twist.

And we meet, with
Champagne and a chicken at last.
—**Mary Wortley Montagu,** *The Lover*

5 CHAPTER

the foods of love

Linda Piggott, who was chef to the British Ambassador to the United Nations, once said, "If it doesn't go with Champagne, it's not meant to be eaten!" But ask a dozen people which foods go best with Champagne cocktails and you might get a dozen different answers. The truth is, Champagne is the only beverage other than water that can flawlessly accompany every course from hors d'oeuvres to dessert.

Serious connoisseurs—even fictitious ones—order everything from bruts to rosés to accompany all sorts of entrées. For example, in Ian Fleming's novel, *Diamonds Are Forever*, British superspy James Bond savored the joys of simple repasts like "a quarter bottle of Bollinger, a chafing dish containing four small slivers of steak on toast canapés, and a small bowl of sauce [béarnaise]." The great Auguste Escoffier was not the only chef to match his creations with Champagne instead of chardonnay or Chablis. Grand establishments such as "21" and Le Cirque in Manhattan have been not only serving their patrons glasses of Champagne with their signature dishes, but cooking with it, as well. But you don't have to be a culinary elitist or a millionaire connoisseur to savor this fabulous combination at breakfast, lunch, dinner, or dessert.

Breakfast or Brunch

Some people start their day with a cup of coffee and a bowl of cold cereal. Others prefer more jolting starters like wheat germ, raw eggs, and yogurt milk shakes. Then there are those who have more style. Master chef Ferdinand Point once shared, "I like to start my day off with a glass of Champagne....It may not be the universal medicine for every disease, as my friends the Champagne people in Reims and Épernay so often tell me, but it does less harm than any other liquid."

When renowned French chef Paul Bocuse first arrived as an apprentice at La Pyramide in Vienne, France, he was responsible for pouring glasses of Champagne for both chef Point and his sous chef. After a few days, the young Bocuse secretly poured himself a serving in a salad bowl. Naturally, he was caught. But to his surprise, he was not reprimanded. The next morning, Bocuse poured Champagne for his superior and set the bottle down. As he turned away, Point stopped him and poured some Champagne in a salad bowl for him. The ritual continued each and every morning for five years.

Other aficionados such as Noël Coward agreed that Champagne at breakfast time lends a sparkle to the day. When asked why he drank Champagne

---

O

There's a good reason why cheese always seems to make an appearance when wine is served. A wine salesman once shared his secret with us: "Buy with apples, sell with cheese." Apples clear the palate, allowing for unimpeded tasting, whereas cheeses are reputed to coat the tongue slightly, masking some of the harsher flavors. Whether this is true or not, there's no denying that cheeses, from brie to stilton, provide a smooth contrast to a Champagne cocktail.

The 1939 New York World's Fair provided Depression-weary Americans with a view of the future as well as the outside world. At the Belgian pavilion, lunchtime attendees could sip an "imported Champagne cocktail" or bask in the refreshing pleasures of a "Fruit Refrachais au Champagne" for an outrageous 75 cents.

for breakfast every morning, Coward casually replied, "Doesn't everyone?"

In fact, Champagne cocktails such as the Buck's Fizz (*see page 37*), Mimosa (*see page 37*), and Poinsettia (*see page 75*) are frequently featured on brunch menus around the world as accompaniments to familiar dishes such as a traditional British breakfast of eggs, bacon, sausage, and grilled tomato; Eggs Benedict smothered in hollandaise sauce; French toast topped with fresh berries; or a bagel topped with smoked salmon, cream cheese, thin slices of red onion, and capers.

Libations such as the French 75 (*see page 46*), Moulin Rouge (*see page 83*), or Sputnik (*see page 73*) can also enhance more exotic breakfast delights such as Chinese dim sum: a variety of steamed or fried dumplings stuffed with meat, seafood, vegetables, sweet bean paste, or preserves. (One of our favorites is called *ch'a-shao-pao*, a steamed bun filled with roasted pork.) This popular form of brunch menu can also contain simple fare such as slices of roast duck, barbecued pork, and ginger chicken or dishes of fried rice and sautéed vegetables.

Chocolate-lovers need not deny themselves their passion in the morning hours either. The Golden Bar (*see page*

According to dietitians at the Mayo Clinic and the U.S. Department of Agriculture, the popular misconception about alcohol being removed during the cooking process is just that: a misconception. Eighty-five percent of the alcohol content of wine or hard liquor remains when added to boiling water (when removed from the heat). Seventy-five percent is left after it's flambéed over food. Forty percent is still present after being baked or simmered for fifteen minutes in a savory or sweet dish. If you wanted to completely remove the alcohol from a sauce or entrée, you have to cook it for about three hours. (But then, would you really want to consume the results?)

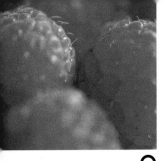

75) is the perfect complement to a truly decadent morning treat—a chocolate breakfast. This unique repast consists of *pain au chocolat* (chocolate croissants), a pot of hot cocoa, and a plate of Swiss chocolates.

Named after Aphrodite, the Greek goddess of love, aphrodisiacs are said to increase an individual's libido. Over the centuries, numerous foods and beverages have been added to this list of supposed sexual stimulants including chocolate, apricots, figs, scallops, honey, okra, ginseng root, almonds, rose petals, peppers, steak, ginger root, and anchovies.
But the pairing of oysters with Champagne has inspired hundreds of stories and scenes on the silver screen—more than all the others combined. Many experts believe the seafood's lascivious texture and the wine's natural inhibition-removers work romantic magic together. In 1989, the U.S. Food and Drug Administration declared that there was no scientific proof that any aphrodisiac worked to treat sexual dysfunction. (Of course, if they ever admitted the truth about aphrodisiacs, there'd be no need for them to continue their research on the subject!)

Lunch

During the dark days of the Second World War (and probably every day thereafter), British Prime Minister Winston Churchill drank Champagne with his midday meal. "A single glass of Champagne imparts a feeling of exhilaration. The nerves are braced, the imagination is stirred, the wits become more nimble," he reasoned.

Obviously, a lunchtime meal accompanied by a Champagne cocktail should consist of more than your average peanut butter on white bread. But the menu doesn't have to be over the top either. California wine producers John and Tracy Anderson note that sparkling wines can be served with turkey or sausages as well as some shockingly American dishes, such as pizza and potato chips. We prefer not to stretch our palates to that extreme (even though Marilyn Monroe did in *The Seven Year Itch*). However, a good old-fashioned turkey-and-bacon club sandwich washed down with a cranberry-laced Métro (*see page 75*) is a natural.

Try pairings such as a Chicago (*see page 75*) with bratwurst, crusty bread, and a romaine salad; an Americana (*see page 70*) with New England clam chowder; a Champagne Bath (*see page 56*) with a Champagne fondue (*this page*); a China Clipper (*see page 78*) with fish and chips; or a Sirius Stargarita (*see page 68*) with a steak and bean taco.

Times have changed since the traditional "21" Steak Tartare was immortalized in the film, *Wall Street* (1987), but this classic plate of raw minced beef and capers—which was singer Dinah Shore's favorite noontime meal—is still as popular as ever. And the Carpaccio served at Harry's Bar has been one of the restaurant's most popular dishes since Giuseppe Cipriani first created it in 1950. This invention was to honor both the Renaissance painter Vittore Carpaccio, whose work was on exhibit in Venice that year, and his regular patron, Contessa Amalia Nani Mocenigo, who had been placed on a diet that forbade her to eat cooked meat. Either dish can be happily married to an Absolutely Fabulous (*see page 63*) or a Moulin Rouge (*see page 83*).

Another favorite "comfort food" combo is a Bolly-Stolly (*see page 85*) and a Croque Monsieur—a French-toasted ham and Swiss cheese sandwich

CHAMPAGNE FONDUE

1 clove garlic
1 lb. ementhal cheese
8 oz. gruyère cheese
1 tbs. cornstarch
1 tsp. lemon juice
1 tsp. kirsch or white rum
1 cup extra dry or brut Champagne
1 pinch black pepper
1 pinch white pepper
1 sourdough baguette

Split the clove of garlic in half lengthwise. Rub the inside of the fondue pot with it, then discard garlic. Grate the cheeses and mix them in the pot. Add cornstarch and lemon juice. Stir over medium heat on the stove until the cheese melts. Stir in kirsch and two-thirds of the Champagne. Add black and white pepper. Stir until the mixture becomes thick and creamy. Just before serving, warm the remaining Champagne in a separate saucepan, and stir it into the fondue. Cut the baguette into chunks for dipping, and serve.

STEAK AU CHAMPAGNE

2 8 oz. New York strip steaks
4 tbs. green peppercorns, cracked
2 tbs. all-purpose flour
1 tbs. olive oil
3 tbs. butter
2 tbs. minced garlic
1 minced shallot
1 pinch ground ginger
8 cremini mushrooms, sliced
5 oz. Champagne

Sprinkle steaks with peppercorns. Use the side of a chef's knife or the bottom of a plate to lightly embed the peppercorns into the meat. Flip the steaks and do the same to the other side, then dust both sides lightly with flour. Heat the oil in a large frying pan over medium-high heat. Melt 1tbs. butter in the oil, then add the steaks. Sauté for 3 to 5 minutes. Then turn and sauté for an additional 2 to 4 minutes. Remove steaks from pan and add the minced garlic and shallot. Stir constantly until the garlic begins to turn golden. Add 2 tbs. butter, ginger, mushrooms, and the Champagne. Continue stirring and reduce heat to low. Simmer for 4 to 5 minutes, or until the sauce is reduced by about half. Sauce should still be thin when ready. Spoon sauce over each steak and serve immediately with either steamed vegetables or a grilled tomato.

that's seasoned with Dijon mustard and Worcestershire sauce, dipped in beaten egg yolk and fried in extra virgin olive oil. It's a lunchtime specialty at Harry's Bar in Venice, at French Roast in Manhattan, and just about every bistro in Paris.

Dinner

Before dinner, the classic Champagne Cocktail (*see page 28*) has held court as the ultimate aperitif for nearly a century—except in France, where the Kir Royale (*see page 44*) reigns supreme. But even an appetite-enhancing Du Monde (*see page 76*) or Keuka Cup (*see page 78*) can be paired with classics such as buckwheat blinis (rich egg pancakes) topped with crème fraîche and caviar, pâté de maison, or raw oysters. These same libations can also be combined with more unique first courses like sushi, spicy samosas, or crostini.

Entreés such as poached salmon topped with a raspberry-orange glaze or a rich hollandaise sauce, grilled lamb chops stuffed with fresh mint and pignolas, or medallions of beef tenderloin served with a béarnaise sauce can be accompanied by a palate-pleasing brut, a sensuous White's Club (*see page 68*), or an Imperial Duo (*see page 80*). A special match is a roasted leg of lamb crusted in garlic paired with a Champagne Julep (*see page 43*).

Champagne risotto, featuring fresh porcinis and shallots or fresh scallops and scallions, is a rich, delicate treat that can be paired with an original Cold Duck (*see page 68*).

Champagne can also be used in the dishes themselves. One of our favorite creations is Steak au Champagne (*see facing page*) which combines oyster mushrooms, shallots, and Champagne into a delicate sauce that's served over steak au poivre vert. Manhattan's "21" offers patrons a smoked salmon and trout appetizer that's lightly tossed in a shallot-and-Champagne vinaigrette and topped with a light drizzle of chive oil. The same Champagne and shallot base is also featured in their signature blue cheese and walnut dressing and their citrus ginger dressing.

Dessert

One of the grand rules of wine and food is that with complimentary (as opposed to contrasting) flavors, the dessert should never be sweeter than the wine. Thus, a wide variety of Champagne cocktails make ideal accompaniments to after-dinner sweets (especially those which incorporate dessert wines and liqueurs). Desserts to enjoy with

CHAMPAGNE ZABAGLIONE

5 egg yolks
1 cup sugar
1 cup Champagne

Combine the yolks and sugar in a large stainless steel mixing bowl. Blend thoroughly with a wire whisk and rest over a pot of hard-boiling water. As it begins to warm, beat with a wire whisk until light and foamy. Add the Champagne and continue beating for about 15 minutes until the mixture until thick and creamy. Serve in small bowls, topped with fresh strawberries.

Champagne cocktails include white chocolate crème brulée with a Nelson's Blood (see page 64) or a White's Club (see page 68). Half the fun of making brulée at home is caramelizing the sugar with a blow torch in front of your guests.) Try fresh peach and raspberry compote served with an Americana (see page 70) or a raspberry-peppermint sorbet with a Lynette (see page 75). Chocolate fondue or fresh-baked pecan tarts are great when matched with either a Golden Bar (see page 75) or a Golden Passion (see page 75), but they are equally enticing with a Sputnik (see page 73) or a La Vie en Rose (see page 68).

Naturally, there are some impressive desserts that incorporate Champagne into the actual dish, such as chocolate truffles flavored with Champagne, Strawberries Romanoff, créme champenoise (a favorite at the University of Reims), Champagne Niederdorf (a cocktail-like mèlange of sorbet, strawberries, and rosé Champagne) and Champagne Zabaglione with fresh berries (see page 93).

Party Foods

The first rule of cocktail parties is that with drink there must be food. No one likes to drink on an empty stomach, and your guests will soon be filtering out the door to the nearest restaurant or the next party. The second rule is that the food must be good. It

doesn't have to be expensive, or complex, or served in vast varieties—just good.

Here are a few simple suggestions for a range of interesting nibbles to get you started:

- papadums with chutney (far more impressive than chips and dip, and nearly as simple)
- fresh figs (simply slice them in half)
- bite-sized slices of chilled steak on crackers with a touch of mustard or béarnaise sauce (cook a steak or two the night before, then let them chill in the fridge)
- caviar (it may be expensive, but it's incredibly easy to serve, just open the tin)
- asparagus vinaigrette (steam, chill, drizzle dressing, put on plate, garnish with black sesame seeds if you're going all out)
- paté served with baguette slices

An easy way to estimate the necessary number of appetizers is to calculate that each person will consume two or three of each type of five different hors d'oeuvres in two hours. Remember that the size of the appetizers, the size of the guests, and the size of your budget are factors in either increasing or decreasing the total number needed.

We might tell of breakfasts, and of suppers, suddenly converted from Saharas of intolerable dullness into oases of smiles and laughter by the appearance of Champagne.
—Charles Tovey

Before I was born my mother was in great agony of spirit and in a tragic situation. She could take no food except iced oysters and Champagne. If people ask me when I began to dance, I reply "in my mother's womb, probably as a result of the oysters and Champagne—the food of Aphrodite."
—Isadora Duncan

Ever wonder how some people stay so calm when they're entertaining? There's one secret that every good host knows instinctively. Keep a backup supply of non-perishable party foods stashed away in a cupboard. Think of it as emergency party rations. Water crackers, melba toast, tinned popcorn shrimp (combine them with a little mayo and a squeeze of lemon, place on toast rounds, sprinkle with paprika, and you've got an instant hors d'oeuvre), Terra Chips, frozen mini-quiches and potstickers, cashews, artichoke hearts, olives, goldfish crackers, cornichons, and perhaps a bag of Chinese fortune cookies.

With a well-stocked cupboard, you'll be able to settle comfortably into bed at night, safe in the knowledge that if unexpected guests arrive two hours after you've fallen asleep, at least you'll be able to lay out some food and drinks before you toss them out.

Don't bother with churches, government buildings or city squares. If you want to know about a culture, spend a night in its bars.
—Ernest Hemingway

6 CHAPTER *happy hour*

FABULOUS PLACES TO DRINK CHAMPAGNE

O

While any good bartender can make a delicious Champagne cocktail, great ones are much harder to find. The following is a list of recommendations. While it is by no means a complete guide, it should help you get started on your search and even help you find suitable refuge while you're traveling.

UNITED STATES

Arizona

DIFFERENT POINT OF VIEW

Pointe-Hilton at Tapatio Cliffs, 11111 N. Seventh Street, Phoenix (602/866-7500).

WINDOWS ON THE GREEN

The Phoenician Resort, 6000 Camelback Road, Scottsdale (602/423-2530).

California—Northern

BIX RESTAURANT & LOUNGE

65 Gold Street, San Francisco (415/433-6300).

BUBBLE LOUNGE

714 Montgomery Street, San Francisco (415/434-4204). The west coast version of the Manhattan Champagne bar.

CHEMIN DE FER

518 F Street, Eureka (707/441-9292).

GREYSTONE RESTAURANT

2555 Main Street, St. Helena (707/967-1010). The Culinary Institute of America's dining room housed in a former monastic winery.

HARRY DENTON'S STARLIGHT ROOM

Sir Francis Drake Hotel, 450 Powell Street, San Francisco (415/395-8595). A rooftop nightclub featuring a dance floor and a magnificent view.

JACK'S

615 Sacramento Street, San Francisco (415/421-7355). The landmark lunch spot of Louis Lourie, Alfred Hitchcock, and the city's financial wizards.

LA COLONIAL

20 Cosmo Place, San Francisco (415/931-3600).

LOBBY LOUNGE

The Ritz-Carlton Hotel, 600 Stockton Street, San Francisco (415/296-7465). A luxurious establishment which offers a Royal Tea that includes a Champagne cocktail from 2:30 to 5:00 PM daily.

RUBICON

558 Sacramento Street, Sacramento (415/434-4100).

TRADER VIC'S

9 Anchor Drive, Emeryville (510/653-3400). This is the original Polynesian hideaway which opened its doors in 1934.

TRA VIGNE

1050 Charter Oak Avenue, St. Helena (707/963-4444).

California—Southern

BAR MARMOT

The Chateau Marmot, 8221 Sunset Boulevard, Hollywood (323/656-1010). Hotel bar in a renovated 1920s Hollywood landmark.

C BAR & RESTAURANT

8442 Wilshire Boulevard, Beverly Hills (323/782-8157).

LES DEUX CAFÉ

1638 North Las Palmas, Los Angeles (323/465-0509).

LUCQUES

8474 Melrose Avenue, Los Angeles (323/655-6277).

THE PENINSULA BEVERLY HILLS

9882 Little Santa Monica Boulevard, Beverly Hills (310/551-2888).

POLO LOUNGE
Beverly Hills Hotel & Bungalows, 9641 Sunset Boulevard, Beverly Hills (310/276-2251).

RITZ-CARLTON LAGUNA NIGUEL
One Ritz Carlton Drive, Dana Point (714/240-2000).

SKY BAR
The Mondrian Hotel, 8440 Sunset Boulevard, Los Angeles (323/848-6025).

Florida

JIMMY'Z AT THE FORGE
432 Arthur Godfrey Road, Miami Beach (305/604-9798).

SMITH & WOLLENSKY
1 Washington Avenue, South Point Park, Miami Beach (305/673-2800).

Georgia

BONE'S RESTAURANT
3130 Piedmont Road, Atlanta (404/237-2663).

THE DINING ROOM
The Ritz-Carlton Buckhead, 3434 Peachtree Road NE, Atlanta (404/237-2700).

Illinois

AMBRIA
2300 Lincoln Park West, Chicago (773/472-5959).

BISTRO 110
110 E. Pearson Street, Chicago (312/266-3110).

NARCISSE CHAMPAGNE SALON & CAVIAR BAR
710 N. Clark Street, Chicago (312/787-2675). An intimate, pillow-strewn lounge that even has curtained-off booths.

PARK AVENUE CAFÉ
199 East Walton Street, Chicago (312/944-4414).

POPS FOR CHAMPAGNE
2934 N. Sheffield Avenue, Chicago (773/472-1000). A huge establishment that features a Cigar Yard and Sunday jazz brunches.

Kentucky

LILLY'S RESTAURANT
1147 Bardstown Road, Louisville (502/451-0447).

THE OAKROOM
The Seelback Hilton, 500 Fourth Avenue, Louisville (502/585-3200).

Louisiana

BRENNAN'S RESTAURANT
417 Royal Street, New Orleans (504/525-9711).

THE GRILL ROOM
Windsor Court Hotel, 300 Gravier Street, New Orleans (504/522-1992).

Massachusetts

BIBA RESTAURANT
272 Boylston Street, Boston (617/426-7878).

BLANTYRE
Blantyre Road, Lenox (413/637-3556).

THE DINING ROOM
The Ritz-Carlton Hotel, 15 Arlington Street, Boston (617/536-5700).

Michigan

THE RATTLESNAKE CLUB
300 River Place, Detroit (313/567-4400).

Nevada

BELLAGIO RESORT & CASINO

Las Vegas Boulevard and Flamingo Road, Las Vegas (888/987-6667). The world's largest and most luxurious casino that boasts over 100 bars and branches of famous Manhattan eateries such as Le Cirque 2000.

New York

ASIA DE CUBA

237 Madison Avenue, New York (212/726-7755). Home of the Mambo King.

BOND STREET

6 Bond Street, New York (212/777-2500).

BUBBLE LOUNGE

228 West Broadway, New York (212/431-3433). A Tribeca cocktail lounge with over 300 Champagnes on the menu.

CHAMPAGNE'S

20 W. 55 Street, New York (212/639-9460).

CLEMENTINE

One Fifth Avenue, New York (212/253-0003).

FLUTE

205 W. 54 Street, New York (212/265-5169).

HARRY CIPRIANI

781 Fifth Avenue, New York (212/753-5566). This is the American branch of the original Venetian restaurant and bar.

HARRY CIPRIANI/DOWNTOWN

376 West Broadway, New York (212/343-0999).

MERCER KITCHEN

The Mercer Hotel, 99 Prince Street, New York (212/966-5454).

MONZÚ

142 Mercer Street, New York (212/343-0333).

TORCH

137 Ludlow Street, New York (212/228-5151).

VANDAM

150 Varick Street, New York (212/352-9090).

WINDOWS ON THE WORLD

1 World Trade Center, 107th Floor, New York (212/524-7000).

Ohio

THE REFECTORY

1092 Bethel Road, Columbia (614/451-9774).

SAMMY'S

1400 West 10th Street, Cleveland (216/532-5560).

Pennsylvania

LA BEC-FIN

1523 Walnut Street, Philadelphia (215/567-1000).

STRIPED BASS

1500 Walnut Street, Philadelphia (215/732-4444).

South Carolina

CEDAR GROVE PLANTATION

1365 Highway 25 North, Edgefield (803/637-3056).

Texas

BRENNAN'S RESTAURANT

3300 Smith Street, Houston (713/522-9711).

THE FRENCH ROOM

Adolphus Hotel, 1321 Commence Street, Dallas (214/742-8200).

THE MANSION ON TURTLE CREEK

2821 Turtle Creek Boulevard, Dallas (214/559-2100).

Utah

MARIPOSA

Silver Lake Lodge, Deer Valley/Park City (435/645-6715).

TREE ROOM

Sundance Resort, Sundance (801/223-4200).

Washington

OLIVER'S

Mayflower Park Hotel, 405 Olive Way, Seattle (206/623-8700). An elegant Edwardian room that is also the home of the Seattle Martini Competition.

THE GARDEN COURT

Four Seasons Olympic Hotel, 411 University, Seattle (206/621-1700).

KATHY CASEY FOOD STUDIOS

5130 Ballard Avenue NW, Seattle (206/784-7840). Although not a restaurant, this consultancy specializes in restaurant concept as well as food and beverage recipe development.

Virginia

TUSCARORA MILL

203 Harrison Street SE, Leesburg (703/771-9300).

CANADA
British Columbia

DELILAH'S

1739 Comox Street (in the Denman Place Mall), Vancouver (604/687-3424). A decadently chic West End restaurant, featuring intimate tables and cozy, private dining booths.

GERARD LOUNGE

The Sutton Place Hotel, 845 Burrard Street, Vancouver (604/682-5511). An elegant dark-oak paneled hotel lounge styled like a gentlemen's club.

PICCOLO MONDO

850 Thurlow Street, Vancouver (604/688-1633). A Piedmont-style Italian restaurant with a deep wine list and an excellent sparkling wine aperitif.

EUROPE
Great Britain

AMERICAN BAR

The Savoy Hotel, The Strand, London (011-44-171-836-4343). The place where mixologist Harry Craddock held court during the 1920s and 1930s.

ATHENAEUM HOTEL

116 Piccadilly, London (011-44-171-499-3464).

BIBENDUM RESTAURANT

Michelin House, 81 Fulham Road, London (011-44-171-581-5817).

THE BURLINGTON BAR

Le Meridien Hotel, 21 Piccadilly, London (011-44-171-734-8000).

THE CONNAUGHT HOTEL

Carlos Place, London (011-44-171-499-7070).

DORCHESTER HOTEL

Park Lane, London (011-44-171-629-8888). One of Noël Coward's many homes away from home.

THE RITZ HOTEL

150 Piccadilly, London (011-44-171-493-8181). The finest place to take afternoon tea in all of London.

WINDOWS TO THE WORLD

London Hilton on Park Lane, 22 Park Lane, London (011-44-171-493-8000).

GATSBY CLUB

Wimbledon, Engineers Way, Middlesex (011-44-181-795-2222). The lounge has a great view of the world-famous tennis courts.

France

ALAIN DUCASSE

59 Avenue Raymond Poincaré, Paris (011-33-1-47-27-12-27).

HARRY'S NEW YORK BAR

5 Rue Danau, 2e, Paris (011-33-1-42-61-71-14). A Lost Generation landmark in the Opera district.

HOTEL DU CAP EDEN ROC

Boulevard Kennedy, Cap d'Antibes (011-33-4-93-61-39-01). The place where the stars flock for post-screening cocktails during the Cannes Film Festival.

LES CRAYERES

64 Boulevard Henry-Vasnier, Reims (011-33-3-26-82-80-80).

TAILLEVENT

15 Rue Lamennais, Paris (011-33-1-44-95-15-01).

WILLI'S WINE BAR

13 Rue des Petits-Champs, Paris (011-33-1-42-61-05-09).

Germany

GREEN DOOR

Winterfeldtstrasse 50, Berlin (011-39-1-215-25-15). Offers a signature drink that combines lime juice, brown sugar, fresh mint, and champagne.

Italy

ENOTECA PINCHIORRI

87 Via Ghilbellina, Florence (011-39-55-242-777).

FOUR SEASONS HOTEL

Via Gesù, 8, Milan (011-39-2-77088)

HARRY'S BAR

Calle Vallaresso, San Marco, Venice (011-319-41-528-57-77). A landmark café situated near the Plaza San Marco.

PAPA GIOVANNI

Via dei Sediari 4, Rome (011-39-68-804-807).

Russia

COSMOS

35 Second Line, Vasilievsky Island, Saint Petersburg (011-7-812-327-7256).

ASIA & AUSTRALIA

China

BEIJING HOTEL & CHAMPAGNE BAR

Hu Jia Lou, Chao Yang Qu, Beijing (011-86-10-6501-8888).

Australia

THE CONSERVATORY

Crown Towers, 8 Whiteman Street, Southbank, Melbourne (011-61-3-9292-8888).

producers of champagne
and sparkling wines

There are an incredible number of sparkling wine producers around the world, from tiny single-vineyard boutique wineries where only a few hundred cases are produced in the best years to massive corporations that make enough in a month to fill all the bathtubs in Cleveland.

Prices can range from a few dollars to a few hundred for a bottle, and the most expensive is not always the best. Even within a single winery, a vintage wine may not be superior to the non-vintage. So how do you spot a good bottle at a good price? Practice. Try new ones every chance you get.

We've provided the following list of reputable and renowned producers from France, the United States, Italy, Spain, Australia, New Zealand, South Africa, and Germany with wines in all price ranges. We'd make specific recommendations, but we're still sipping our way through the list and wouldn't want to comment until we've tried them all.

We've included pronunciations for the French wines, as we've found they're much easier to order if you know how to pronounce them.

France

There are well over 150 Champagne producers headquartered in this small northern region. Here's the "short list" of the top Champagne producers accompanied by the correct pronunciation of each house's name:

Ayala (pronounced: "eye-a-la")
Besserat de Bellefon (pronounced: "bess-er-ah deh bell-fon")
Canard-Duchêne (pronounced: "cah-nar doo-chen")
Charles Heidsieck (pronounced: "hide-sick")
Deutz (pronounced: "doots")
Gosset (pronounced: "goss-ay")
Heidsieck Monopole (pronounced: "hide-sick mo-no-pole")
Henriot (pronounced: "hen-ree-oh")
Bollinger (pronounced: "bowl-ahn-jay")
Joseph Perrier (pronounced: "pair-ee-ay")
Krug (pronounced: "kroog")
Lanson (pronounced: "lan-son")
Laurent-Perrier (pronounced: "low-raunt pair-ee-ay")
Louis Roederer (pronounced: "lou-ee rode-er-er")
Mercier (pronounced: "mare-cee-ay")
Moët & Chandon (pronounced: "mow-ette ay shan-don")
Mumm (pronounced: "moom")
Perrier-Jouët (pronounced: "pair-ee-ay joo-ette")
Piper-Heidsieck (pronounced: "piper hide-sick")
Pol Roger (pronounced: "pole row-jay")
Pommery (pronounced: "pom-mer-ay")
Ruinart (pronounced: "roo-ee-nar")
Salon (pronounced: "sall-on")
Taittinger (pronounced: "tay-taun-jay")
Veuve Clicquot (pronounced: "vehv klee-coe")

United States

American wineries produce sparkling wines according to a number of different processes, such as *mèthode champenoise*, *charmat*, continuous (bulk process), or carbonation method. The producers themselves are concentrated in four states. These include:

Argyle (Oregon)
Cordoniu Napa (California)
Domaine Carneros (California)
Domaine Chandon (California)
Domaine Ste. Michelle (Washington)
Glenora (New York)
Gloria Ferrar (California)
Handley (California)
Iron Horse (California)
J Wine Company (California)
Korbel (California)
Mumm Cuvée Napa (California)
Pacific Echo (California)
Piper-Sonoma (California)
Roederer Estate (California)
S. Anderson (California)
Scharffenberger (California)
Schramsberg (California)
Ste. Chapelle (Idaho)
Tribaut (California)

Italy

Spumante and prosecco are the primary varieties of sparkling wine produced in Italy. However, there are other specialities such as sparkling Verdicchio and Barbera wines. Italy's most famous sparkling wine producers, the type of wine each creates, and the region in which it is grown are in the following list:

Asti Spumante (spumante / Piedmont)
Attilo Fabrini (spumante / Marches)
Ca' del Bosco (spumante / Lombardy)
Calissano (spumante / Piedmont)
Catina Sociale Val di Nevola (spumante / Marches)

Ever wonder why some sparkling wines are so expensive, and some aren't? It's not because of some conspiracy. Taxes and tariffs aside, the price has more to do with the manufacture than anything else. There are many methods for putting the sparkle into sparkling wine:

MÉTHODE CHAMPENOISE
(a.k.a. méthode traditionale)

Production takes a year to three years, and the entire process requires constant handling and attention. (In France, the entire process is strictly dictated by regional laws.) The wine goes through a second fermentation in the bottle, where natural carbonation cannot escape and dissolves into the wine.

CHARMAT

The wine is fermented under pressure in huge vats, and then bottled under pressure. The entire process can take up to eight months. In France, this particular wine cannot be called Champagne. In the States it is sometimes labeled as "bulk process."

CONTINUOUS

The grape juice is moved through a series of fermentation and filtration tanks. Yeast and sugar are pumped in at specified points, ensuring that the wine is ready in less than a month.

CARBONATION (a.k.a. gazéifié)

In France, this wine is referred to as *vin de pompe bicyclette* (bicycle pump wine). The wine is injected with carbonation, just like Dr. Pepper. This process can produce a wine that will pop a cork in less than a minute. (Legend has it that a piece of dry ice the size of a pea sealed inside a bottle of ordinary white wine overnight will produce similarly mediocre flavor and sparkle.)

Càvit/Cantina Viticoltori Trento (firmanto champenoise, spumante, and trentino / Trentino-Alto Adige)
Càvit/Cantina Viticoltori Trento (trentino / Trentino-Alto Adige)
Cinzano (spumante / Piedmont)
Garofoli (sparkling Verdicchio and spumante / Marches)
Marchesi Antinori (spumante / Tuscany)
Moscato d'Asti Spumanti (spumante / Piedmont)
Prosecco de Conegliano-Valdobbiadene (prosecco/Veneto region)
Santa Maria della Versa (spumante / Lombardy)
Valentino (spumante / Piedmont)
Venegazzù (spumante / Veneto)
Verdicchio del Castelli di Jesi (sparkling Verdicchio / Marches)

Spain

Produced according to a very similar process employed in the top Champagne wine houses (specifically, *mèthode champenoise*), the sparkling wines (known as *cavas*) developed in Catalonia—a region in northern Spain—include:

Bodega José L. Ferrer (Catalonia)
Bodegas J. Freixadas (Catalonia)
Cavas de Ampurdan (Catalonia)
Cavas del Ampurdán (Catalonia)
Cavas Mascaró (Catalonia)
Codorníu (Catalonia)
Freixenet (Catalonia)
Juvé y Camps (Catalonia)
Marqués de Monistrol (Catalonia)
Segura Viudas (Catalonia)

Australia, New Zealand, & South Africa

Only a small handful of Australian, New Zealand, and South African wineries have attempted to cultivate the Chardonnay, Pinot Noir, and Pinot Meunier grapes to Champagne-style blends and to bottle their own lines of sparkling wines. These include:

Bergkelder, The (South Africa)
Cellier Le Brun (New Zealand)
Chateau Remy (Australia)
Clos Cabrière (South Africa)

De Bertoli (Australia)
Hungerford Hill (Australia)
Nederburg (South Africa)
Penfolds (Australia)
Simonsig (South Africa)
Villiera (South Africa)

Germany

German sparkling wine (which is known as *sekt*) is produced by a number of houses in response to a centuries-old demand for this particular style of wine. These are:

Christian Adalbert Kupferberg
Deinhard & Co.
Eltville
Faber Sektkellerei Faber
Fürst von Metternich
Henkell & Co.
Johannisberg
Koblenz
Mainz
Matheus Müller
Peter Herres
Schloss Böchingen
Schloss Saarfels
Sektkellerei Spicka
Serrig/Saar
Trier
Wiesbaden

Credits

Photos on pages i, ii–iii, iv–v, vi–vii, viii, x, xiii, 7, 10, 12, 13, 14, 17, 20–21, 29, 38, 45, 50, 57, 61, 65, 69, 78, 82, 91, and 99 (c) P.R. Brown /Bau-Da Design.

Photos on pages 8, 24–25, 26, 34, 41, 42, 48–49, 52, 55, 58–59, 71, 72, 77, 85, 86, 89, 93, 94–95, 97, 103, 104 (c) Jared M. Brown / Miller-Brown.

Photos on pages 47, 74, and 81 (c) John Kuczala / John Kuczala Photography.

Photos on pages 22 and 98 (c) Courtney Winston / Courtney Grant Winston Photography.

Photos on pages xiv and 1 provided courtesy of Balzac Communications.

Photos on pages 3 and 4 provided courtesy of Maisons Marques & Domaines USA, Inc.

Photos on pages 31 and 62 provided courtesy of Margaret Stern Communications.

Photo on page 66–67 provided courtesy of Vranken America.

The bottle-and-glass illustration on pages 28, 32-33, 34, 35, 38, 41, 42, 44, 53, 54, 56, 63, 64, 68, 70, 73, 75, 76, 80, and 83 (c) Jared M. Brown / Miller-Brown.

Acknowledgments

We'd like to propose a toast to a number of people who advised, aided, and abetted us in creating this book. Three cheers to our editor Jeremie Ruby-Strauss for encouraging us once again and our publisher Judith Regan for having faith. Cheers to the team at ReganBooks who make our work possible, especially André Becker, Robin Arzt, Maggie McMahon, Kate Stark, Robert Stroud, and John Wing.

A raised Champagne flute to Jean-Louis Carbonnier of the Champagne Wines Information Bureau for providing facts and anecdotes about the world's favorite wine; Captain Peter Murison of Buck's Club in London for telling us the story of the Buck's Fizz; Sandra Bernier at Jack's in San Francisco for relating the Mimosa story; Steve and the gang at the Idaho Baseball Academy in Boise for allowing us to pitch a few corks on New Year's Eve; Judy Ahola at the Sutton Place Hotel in Vancouver for digging up the sabering instructions; Valerie-Anne Rouzineau at Stern Communications for introducing us to Lillet Rouge; and John Caruso of Goldenbärr for introducing us to chocolate vodka.

We'd like to thank Baccarat, Inc., Crystal St. Louis, and Riedel for the use of their beautiful glassware; Todd Wasserman, Haim Hassin, and all the folks at Piper-Heidsieck and Remy Amerique; Jim Heckler at *The Globe*; as well as Jonny Santiago, Hamid Rashidazada, and Mario Flores at *Torch*. We also wish to thank Jill Siefert and George Brightman for assisting us with the directory.

Hats off to Kathy Casey, Tony Abu-Ganim, Jeri Banks, Pat Boyd, Debra Holden, the guys at the Bubble Lounge, Pops for Champagne, and the other venues mentioned in this book who provided us with their best recipes. And one last huzzah to photographer and designer P.R. Brown.

Last Call

Anistatia R Miller and Jared M. Brown write about food, drink, and modern iconography. They wrote and designed *Shaken Not Stirred®: A Celebration of the Martini* (HarperPerennial, 1997). They have written for *Wine Spectator, Icon: Thoughtstyle Magazine*, and *Adobe Magazine*. Brown was a judge at the First International Martini Challenge in 1999. Together they have appeared on CBC Radio's *Afternooon Edition* and *Pacific Palate*, *Martini Madness* and *The Best of Food & Wine* in Vancouver. Former Manhattanites and Vancouverites, they currently live in Boise, Idaho. Their Web site *Shaken Not Stirred®: A Celebration of the Martini* earned awards including Web Review, Magellan, Point Survey, and GIST. The site has been expanded to include Champagne cocktails.

Don Gatterdam is Director of Custom Publishing for M. Shanken Communications (publishers of *Wine Spectator*, *Cigar Aficionado*, *Food Arts*, *Market Watch*, and *Hamptons Country* magazines). He serves on the board of the American Institute of Wine and Food (AIWF), which promotes improving the quality and awareness of food and beverages in America. He also serves on the board of directors of the X-Art Foundation, which explores contemporary art and new media. A graduate of the University of California at Santa Cruz, he currently resides in Manhattan.

You can visit them at: http://members.aol.com/Theauthors/